Chestertonian
Calvinism

CHESTER ~TONIAN *Calvinism*

A Brief Explanation and Defense

DOUGLAS WILSON

BLOG & MABLOG
PRESS AND TIRE CENTER
MOSCOW, IDAHO

Blog & Mablog Press and Tire Center
Moscow, Idaho
www.dougwils.com

ISBN: 9798369921944

Version: 20221210PDF

To the memory of Martin Marprelate,
the most Chestertonian of Puritans

Contents

Chesterton's view of the Protestant Reformation was almost entirely negative . . . *Calvinism* and *Puritanism* were among the vilest words in his lexicon. (Ralph Wood, *Chesterton: The Nightmare Goodness of God*, p. 3)

Calvinism is the most non-Christian of Christian systems. (G.K. Chesterton, *Eugenics and Other Evils*)

Foreword

This is not really a book "about" Chesterton, although he figures very largely in it. It is more about the spirit of Chesterton, as combined with a robust understanding of the Godness of God.

For some, the words *Chestertonian* and *Calvinism* are a really bad mismatch, kind of like chocolate and peanut butter, an intuitive conviction that lasts only as long as nobody tries it. Chestertonian Calvinism has not been tried and found wanting, it has been found to have been way too much fun and not tried.

Some of the following chapters will discuss Chesterton directly, and some will address Calvinism directly, but the central theme of the book has to do with a third thing. That is what I would call the exuberant romance of orthodoxy, an orthodoxy best represented by gents like John Owen and Francis Turretin and Charles Hodge. This is not to say that Turretin was a laugh riot exactly, but it is to say that when free grace gets loose among the people, one of the things that happens is that some freed people get loose among the people also. A certain breed of thinker becomes *possible*.

If we are being honest with one another, as I suppose we should, there may be places where the chapters that follow meander somewhat, but I have done my level best to make it seem like this was done on purpose. Another name for this book could be something like "Things I Have Thought About after Reading Chesterton."

I am driving at one central point, which is that liberating grace should actually liberate. There have been times in history when it has done so, and consequently the keepers of dignified religion have always done their best to try to get the ensuing rowdiness back into the box. One of their tricks is to rename and reframe those who successfully got out of their box, and sometimes this trick works. Sometimes it even works on someone as liberated as Chesterton, such that he takes on certain false assumptions about some of his more liberated brothers.

So be advised that the argument of the book does not unfold like a Monarch butterfly unfolding from a chrysalis but is rather more like a moth taking fifteen runs or so at the same light bulb. Addressed (in various ways) will be the importance of a Chestertonian spirit when reading history, when writing novels or poetry, when evaluating evolution, when discussing Roman Catholicism, when working through what Father Brown would have made of the Shroud, in considering how Chesterton admired Bunyan, when defending the West, and when going to bed tired at the end of it all. If books about Chesterton were soups, this one would be a mulligatawny.

Too much Chesterton without the bedrock of God's sovereignty will eventually just turn the reader into a wannabe Oscar Wilde. Too much Calvinism, without the exuberant liveliness that comes from writers like Chesterton, will turn the reader into three hundred pounds of wet sand,

and no fun at all at parties. Not wanting either of these outcomes, we turn with increasing interest to the following pages.

Douglas Wilson
Christ Church, 2022

Make Definitions Great Again

I n writing a book like this, it is incumbent upon the person who initially thought it was a good idea, usually the author, to define his terms. What is meant by Chestertonian? And what is meant by Calvinism?

This will all get filled out as we work through the journey that is this book, but think of this brief chapter as taking a glance at the map before hopping in the car. For those born after the turn of the last century, maps are folded papers we used to glance at before hopping into cars. Now we just let our phones boss us around. But we are not going to go through this small book in that way, we are not traveling the way of the phone—"go through this light, and turn left at the next one, which will be green when you get there." The reason is that, while you *do* arrive at your destination this way, you have no idea how it all happened, or how many algorithms were involved, and consequently you do not have a clear mental picture of what is actually going on.

As a result, I am proposing that I define my terms here. By *Chestertonian* I am talking about an ongoing spirit of exuberant gratitude, a spirit that enables the person in possession of it to look at the world in ways that strike others as new, fresh, paradoxical, or just plain sideways.

Here is Chesterton on gratitude.

> I would maintain that thanks are the highest form of thought, and that gratitude is happiness doubled by wonder.

Chesterton's fame regarding his use of paradox was not the result of a mere verbal cleverness. The ability to tumble words around is not limited to believers. Oscar Wilde was a wit also, but the wit did not go all the way down to bedrock. With Chesterton it did, and that bedrock was gratitude.

> You say grace before meals. All right. But I say grace before the concert and the opera, and grace before the play and pantomime, and grace before I open a book, and grace before sketching, painting, swimming, fencing, boxing, walking, playing, dancing and grace before I dip the pen in the ink.

This is right and proper. Scripture tells us to give thanks *in* everything. "In every thing give thanks: for this is the will of God in Christ Jesus concerning you" (1 Thess. 5:18). On top of that, we are told to give thanks *for* everything. "Giving thanks always for all things unto God and the Father in the name of our Lord Jesus Christ" (Eph. 5:20). Chesterton's gratitude for everyday stuff was palpable, and he wrote in such a way as to make outsiders hungry to participate in it with him. It is one of the central reasons for his durability as a writer—it is his stand-out quality. Refusal to murmur like Israelites in the wilderness is something that shines like a bright light in a very dark place.

> Do all things without murmurings and disputings: That ye may be blameless and harmless, the sons of God, without rebuke, in the midst of a crooked and perverse nation, *among whom ye shine as lights* in the world. (Phil. 2:14–15)

But such a consistent spirit of gratitude actually has a few theological prerequisites, whether acknowledged by the grateful saint or not. And that brings us to the next term from my title that I need to define.

By *Calvinism*, I am using the term in its modern usage, meaning that I am talking about the sovereignty of God in all things, and particularly in the matter of salvation. To echo the words of Westminster, God freely and unalterably ordains whatsoever comes to pass, and He does so in a way that does not hinder or interfere with the liberty of the creature, but rather establishes it. When this general statement of truth is applied to whether or not Smith will repent and turn to Christ, the rest of the Calvinistic understanding of soteriology follows. Man in his fallen estate is not able to save himself and is not even able to prepare himself to be saved by another. Consequently, God the Father elected those who would come to believe in Him, God the Son laid down His life in order to secure the salvation of those same individuals, and God the Holy Spirit quickened them at the time when they were to be converted. As a result of the work that only God could begin, the Spirit has guaranteed that He will finish and complete that same work, ensuring that all such converted individuals will persevere in holiness until the end of their lives. This is what I am referring to in this book when I am talking about Calvinism.

Now when it came to the *name* of Calvinism, it has to be said in all honesty that Chesterton simply detested it. He really did not like those Christians who articulated the details of what he, Chesterton, constantly assumed in his posture of gratitude. Those who have been Calvinists for any length of time have run into this all the time. Many believers are formal Arminians, but become Calvinists on their knees, whenever they pray. They ask God to do things that their formal system of theology denies He has anything to do with.

I am reminded of the experience that Greg Bahnsen told me about. He had gone to a minister's prayer breakfast shortly after a big earthquake had rocked LA. The assembled men were told that God doesn't do earthquakes, that His methods do not run in that line, and so on. Never mind what the prophet Amos said about when disaster befalls a city (Amos 3:6). At any rate, after everyone had learned that God doesn't do earthquakes, the gathered ministers went to prayer, and thanked God for when the earthquake had happened—i.e., not in rush hour. God doesn't do earthquakes and is to be gratefully thanked for the timing of it.

Saying grace before everything and anything is an activity that assumes certain things. It assumes that the one you are thanking had something to do with it. I thank the waiter who delivers my food to me . . . I do not shout my thanks across the restaurant at a departing and very startled fellow customer. He had nothing to do with it.

Now of course the comeback is going to be that the problem is caused by the Calvinist insistence that God is sovereign over sin and evil, and not just unobjectionable activities like walking and playing and dancing. But Chesterton could be quite clear-headed about evil . . . he just was not prepared to think that Calvinists were being clear-headed about it also.

Another of Chesterton's peeves was occasioned by the Puritans. The Puritans were Calvinists, of course, but their project involved a lot more than just that. They were world-and-life-view people, and thus their views on God's sovereignty extended into everything—into politics, sports, entertainment, writing, architecture, and so on. Over time, due to the effects of slander and the inexorable effects of wineskins getting old, the Puritans gained a reputation for being, well, puritanical. But by this I mean what that word has come to mean, which would make them the guardians of all forms of pious buzzkill.

The problem is that this sad reality did not really start to unfold until a century or more into the project—it took quite some time before all the blankets got wet.

It follows that nearly every association which now clings to the word *puritan* has to be eliminated when we are thinking of the early Protestants. Whatever they were,

they were not sour, gloomy, or severe; nor
did their enemies bring any such charge
against them . . . For More, a Protestant
was one 'drone of the new must of lewd
lightness of minde and vane gladness of
harte' . . . Protestantism was not too grim,
but too glad, to be true . . . Protestants are
not ascetics but sensualists. (Lewis, *English
Literature*, p. 34)

The hurdle that Lewis urges us to clear when
it comes to the Puritans was a hurdle that Chesterton, for all his greatness, failed to clear.

A Bit about Our Namesake

*T*his short chapter will not so much be a biography of Chesterton, as it will be an admiration of his influence with a small handful of biographical details scattered here and there.

Chesterton was born in 1874 and lived until 1936. His family were occasional Unitarians, which, if you are going to be a Unitarian at all, that's the way to go—although they did have him baptized into the Church of England. He was educated at St. Paul's School, and then attended the Slade School of Art, which he never finished. He did take literature and art courses there.

He was kind of a freelancer but was mostly a newspaperman—he wrote a weekly column for many years. He wrote theology, culture, politics, detective fiction, odd fiction, apologetics, and poetry. He wrote around 80 books, lots of poems, hundreds of short stories, and countless newspaper columns. He was a phenomenon. He was a great doodler. He was a doodler for the ages.

He married Frances Blogg in 1901—she was the one who had been largely responsible for bringing him back to the Anglican Church. Despite Chesterton's great love for kids, they were never able to have children. He was received into the Roman Catholic Church in 1922.

Here is T.S. Eliot on the great man's impact:

> He was importantly and consistently on the side of the angels. Behind the Johnsonian fancy-dress, so reassuring to the British public, he concealed the most serious and revolutionary designs—concealing them by exposure . . . Chesterton's social and economic ideas . . . were fundamentally Christian and

Catholic. He did more, I think, than any man of his time—and was able to do more than anyone else, because of his particular background, development and abilities as a public performer—to maintain the existence of the important minority in the modern world. He leaves behind a permanent claim upon our loyalty, to see that the work that he did in his time is continued in ours.

Consider his timeline. Chesterton was born less than a decade after the close of the American Civil War. Darwinism was still hot and fresh. He saw England's Boer War in South Africa (which he opposed), the First World War, and the Russian Revolution. I like to regard Chesterton as a one-man army, standing (pretty effectively) against what all the cool kids of that generation were dazzled by—eugenics, free love, evolution, scientific hubris, and collectivism. He died three years after the publication of C.S. Lewis's first *Christian* book, which was *The Pilgrim's Regress*. Someone needs to write a short ahistorical sketch of the time the two men met up accidentally in a train station somewhere and had an unrecorded conversation for the ages.

As influential as he was individually, he was also instrumental in the conversion of Lewis, who went on to affect untold millions. Here is Lewis describing some of his final days before his conversion.

> It was here that I first read a volume of Chesterton's essays. I had never heard of him and had no idea of what he stood for; nor can I quite understand why he made such an immediate conquest of me. (*Surprised by Joy*, p. 190)

One of the reasons why Chesterton is such an encouragement to us in our demented times is that he understands the role of the *sane* imagination. This is not the same thing as understanding imagination itself—for no man understands that—but Chesterton does understand the important role that imagination must play. He understands it, and he practices what he understands.

So when Napoleon once said that imagination rules the world—a great aphorism if ever there was one—he was simply giving us some material to work with. In what senses might this be true? In what senses might we get all tangled up in what we falsely think of as imagination?

There is a distinction between the throne of imagination—the human heart and mind—and the realm of imagination—everything else. One of the central reasons we are languishing in our public life is that we have allowed a divorce between the throne and the realm. Artists are assumed to be the custodians of the imagination, but because of their insistence upon complete autonomy, they have become like a mad king who has his run of the throne room, and nothing else. And outside, in the mundane realm of ho-hummer, imagination is assumed to be irrelevant. Imagination looks to be pretty dangerous, to judge from the howls that come from the throne room.

What this means—when Christians finally wake up to the real state of affairs—is that we are besieging a city with no walls and no defenses. If imagination rules the world, perhaps we should focus on getting some.

Chesterton once said, speaking of those who accommodate themselves to the trend of the times, that "at its worst it consists of many millions of frightened creatures all accommodating themselves to a trend that is not there." This is something that I am afraid has happened more than once. It has happened more than once just since Chesterton died.

It is not that hard to spook a herd. The trend is that things are trending. The buffalo set up a self-authenticating feedback loop, and the necessary plan of action seems obvious to them all, and remains such, right over the cliff. But enough about the covid pandemic and lockdown protocols.

But there are contrarians who don't think matters through any more than the stampeders do—and it doesn't much matter what the fad in question is. It might be iPhones, or N.T. Wright fan clubs, or the election of a welterweight like Joe Biden, or a Taylor Swift concert. There are contrarians who are accidentally right when the herd is accidentally wrong, or accidentally wrong when the herd is accidentally right. That's no good either.

We need thoughtful contrarians—principled contrarians, men like Chesterton. When the house of immovability is built on the foundation of pigheadedness, that house is filled with endless quarrels. When the house is built on the foundation of well-spoken conviction, the home is filled with laughter and joy—though storms may rage outside.

In that same place, when Chesterton spoke of those sociologists who spoke of the great need we have to accommodate ourselves to the trend of the time, he noted that, in any given time, the trend of the time *at its best* consists of those who will not accommodate themselves to anything. Athanasius had to stand *contra mundum*, and it is *he* who is the representative man from that era, and not the whole world he had to contend against. *Transit gloria mundi*, with the exception of that courageous glory which was willing to stand up against the glory of all the regnant poohbahs.

Take Chesterton himself as a grand example …

Calvinism
Under Jove

Doctrines bring along more than the content of the doctrine with them. Doctrines have ancestries. Doctrines have histories. Doctrines have connotations that go well beyond their denotations. And to bring all this down to the point, doctrines also develop personalities.

Sometimes that personality is obvious to pretty much everyone, and other times a "personality" is attributed to it unfairly. And then, to make everything a little more festive, some people who subscribe to the doctrine in question will accept that attribution as accurate and do their best to live up to it. Or down to it, as the case may be.

Consider what has been done to the word Puritan. What does the word *puritanical* bring to mind? We think immediately of a stuffed-shirt wowser, with a buckle on his black hat, trying hard to affix a scarlet letter to the blouse of yet another wayward woman.

This is a book about Chestertonian Calvinism, and the phrase will undoubtedly strike many observers as oxymoronic, a contradiction in terms. Not only so, but a contradiction on multiple levels—everybody knows that Calvinists are supposed to be temperamentally dour, our ecclesiastical Eeyore's. This collides with the adjective Chestertonian, and not only so, it also collides with Chesterton himself. We could hunt around for a long time before finding a Christian writer who took a dimmer view of Calvinism than Chesterton did.

But in this I want to argue that Chesterton was at war with himself. This was not the kind of conflict that he might have in real life with his old debating partner, George Bernard Shaw, or the kind of conflict he gloried in through poetry—as in his poem *Lepanto*, where Don John of Austria goes to the war. No, this really is an internal conflict, and Chesterton really has to wrestle with himself.

Now I grant that Chesterton was clever enough to avoid wrestling with himself, and so I propose that somebody should make him. And when I say "somebody," I mean that I would like to undertake the task. But I know the risks involved are great, and I only take the project on because Chesterton has been dead for the better part of a century, and hence his powers are somewhat diminished.

Chesterton was a champion of the common man and exulted in the extraordinary wisdom found in ordinary places. Allow me to mention three areas where Calvinism has excelled in its patronage of the common man as well.

The first area has been in the realm of sabbath-keeping. We are all aware of the hazards posed by fastidious sabbatarians—our Lord collided with *them* more than once, and once modern sabbath-keeping became the norm, it was not long before peck sniffs started to roam the city, putting padlocks on swing sets, lest any antinomian eight-year-olds swing themselves to perdition.

But for the common man, the laboring man, the Sabbath came as a profound relief. And this was the intent of the law as first given.

> Remember the sabbath day, to keep it holy. Six days shalt thou labour, and do all thy work: But the seventh day is the sabbath of the Lord thy God: in it thou shalt not do any work, thou, nor thy son, nor thy daughter, *thy manservant, nor thy maidservant*, nor thy cattle, nor thy stranger that is within thy gates. (Exodus 20:8–10)

We who have grown up with two-day weekends as part of the work week landscape tend to think of sabbatarianism as the kind of pinched attitude that wants to sweep in and prohibit a list of fun activities on one of those two days off. "Put down that frisbee!" But what sabbatarianism actually did was usher in real rest for the downtrodden down at the workhouse. The Sabbath is a true friend of the laboring man.

Music is another area where the Reformation brought sweet relief to ordinary people. The Reformation was not just a doctrinal reformation—it was also liturgical, cultural, political, and musical.

Prior to the Reformation, congregational singing was not really a thing. The people would go to church to function as spectators, with all the real action going on behind the rood screen. The ordained priests were up behind there, doing their thing, and the members of the choir, also clergymen, were the ones who made the music.

But as the Reformation started to get traction, something had to give. And one service on Christmas Day in Basel, the congregation under the ministry of John Oecolampadius, just started singing. The congregation. The *people* started singing.

As this developed, a Genevan Psalter was born. Queen Elizabeth was not pleased—which was something she was good at—and called them "Geneva jigs." They were lively, and syncopated, and the people loved them.

Third example—although it would not be hard to come up with many more than these. What did painting in the medieval period take for its subjects? Well, pretty much anybody with a halo. The holy family, Madonna and child, the twelve apostles, and so on. Now do not take me wrong. I have no problem with art treating biblical themes. That did not go away with the Reformation. But what came in as a result of the Reformation?

The Dutch realist painters introduced us to the glory of the mundane. A girl reading a letter, a woman making lace, another woman pouring something from a jug, a girl with an earring, another girl smirking, still life table settings, an anatomy lecture with a cadaver. In short, art came down and dwelt among the people . . . just as the Lord had done.

And this brings us to our first contact with what I am calling Chestertonian Calvinism. I believe that there was something in the original genius of the Reformation that resonates deeply with a foundational aspect of Chesterton's genius. For various reasons, they have been estranged, but I think we need to work on a reconciliation.

Reformation Calvinism was born under Jove. It flourishes under Jove and is spiritually healthy there. But for the last several centuries (at least) it has come under the baneful influence of Saturn.

For those who dismiss my "pagan tomfoolery"—planetary influences mixed with Christian theology *indeed*—with a sneer and say that *they* want a Calvinism under *Christ*, thank you, the better to enable us to get back to the gospel-preserving debates about supralapsarianism, not to mention how many eggs your wife is allowed to cook on the Lord's Day, several things have to be said.

First, they haven't understood my point. Nobody around here has any sympathy for pagan unbelief and superstition. Christ is Lord, and only Christ. But when my point is misunderstood in this way, folks haven't understood it because they are under the baneful influences of Saturn.

Second, this is not a minor issue. Just as Lucy and Susan wouldn't feel safe around Bacchus unless Aslan was around, I don't feel safe around Calvinists under Saturn. When these precious doctrines of ours are used to perpetuate gloom, severity, introspection, accusations, slander, gnat-strangling, and more, the soul is not safe. It is what gives great souls like Chesterton room to misunderstand the doctrines of grace, which he most certainly did—every chance he got.

Third, the original Protestants, and the Puritans especially, were not at all under Saturn. Here is quote from Lewis that you will encounter more than once in these pages.

> But there is no understanding the period of the Reformation in England until we have grasped the fact that the quarrel between the

Puritans and the Papists was not primarily a quarrel between rigorism and indulgence, and that, in so far as it was, the rigorism was on the Roman side. On many questions, and specially in their view of the marriage bed, the Puritans were the indulgent party; if we may without disrespect so use the name of a great Roman Catholic, a great writer, and a great man, they were much more Chestertonian than their adversaries. (C.S. Lewis, *Selected Literary Essays*, p. 116)

This startling insight from Lewis is what I take as my starting point in pursuing this particular and somewhere peculiar vision.

And fourth, with this as the good news, over the last generation, there have been a number of indications that our saturnine exile may be coming to an end. Many Calvinists are again becoming jovial—which should not be reduced to a willingness to tell the occasional joke. The issue is much deeper than that—we are talking about rich liturgy, robust psalm-singing, laughter and sabbath feasting, exuberant preaching, and all with gladness and simplicity of heart. The winter is breaking. This is not just a thaw but promises to be a real spring.

Chestertonian Calvinism

I n this chapter, before we get to Chesterton proper, we have to set the table with a little Deuteronomy, John Piper, C.S. Lewis, and Jonathan Edwards. I hope the reasons for doing this will become obvious by the end.

When these precious doctrines of ours—referring to the absolute sovereignty of God over all things—are twisted in such a way as to perpetuate gloom, severity, introspection, accusations, slander, gnat-strangling, and more, the soul is never safe. The doctrines of grace, understood for what they are, are doctrines of *gladness*.

But whenever God delivers His people in any remarkable way, as the years go by, whatever new wineskin was involved in it will turn gradually into an old wineskin. Part of this process is that the number of unregenerate people will start to grow, but they are stuck with the vocabulary of the previous great reformation and revival. Grumpy people are stuck with the vocabulary of gladness. This gives them new material to work on, new and challenging material to distort. Given enough time, however, distort it they will.

> And they shall be upon thee for a sign and for a wonder, and upon thy seed for ever. Because thou servedst not the Lord thy God with joyfulness, and with gladness of heart, for the abundance of all things; Therefore shalt thou serve thine enemies which the Lord shall send against thee, in hunger, and in thirst, and in nakedness, and in want of all things: and he shall put a yoke of iron upon thy neck, until he have destroyed thee. (Deut. 28:46–48)

In this chapter of Deuteronomy, the people of Israel are being instructed on the nature of the blessings and curses that will come upon them in accordance with their obedience or disobedience to the covenant. That whole chapter makes for some pretty sobering reading. The blessings are outlined in the first 14 verses. But beginning at verse 15, the bulk of the rest of the chapter is dedicated to a description of the curses that will come down upon them. Not only will God curse them, but He will *rejoice* over their destruction (v. 63). Destroying them will bring Him joy. But right in the middle of all that, in our text, we are told *why* the people of God veered away from the blessings that follow obedience and into the dark world of insanity and disobedience.

It was because, while they had full possession of the blessings, they did not treat them or respond to them *as* blessings. Responding to blessing with *greed* or with *guilt* incurs wrath. The required response was *gratitude*. The curses will therefore rest upon them for a sign and a wonder, and on their descendants as well (v. 46). The reason is then given. They were cursed because they did not serve God with two attitudes of thanksgiving—with joyfulness and with gladness of heart (v. 47). On top of all this, they were not joyful and glad in heart because of *all the stuff* (v. 47). And that is why they will be turned out, consigned to the cruelties of their enemies, to the point of their final destruction (v. 48).

As we will see later, when we come to describe the sin of man, the heart of man really is desperately wicked. Who can understand it (Jer. 17:9)? We really are lifted up out of the mire. But part of this desperate wickedness and confusion can be seen in the refusal to get up when God declares an invitation to do so. We must humble ourselves under the mighty hand of God (1 Pet. 5:6). But if we have humbled ourselves in truth, then we won't kick and squall when He does the next thing, which is to exalt us, lifting us up into gladness. If the humility does not end in gladness and triumph, then the humility did not begin (really) in humility at all. Humility *submits*, and therefore does not insist on groveling permanently.

> Glory and honour are in his presence; Strength *and gladness* are in his place. (1 Chron. 16:27)

And the children of Israel that were present at Jerusalem kept the feast of unleavened bread seven days *with great gladness*: and the Levites and the priests praised the Lord day by day, singing with loud instruments unto the Lord. (2 Chron. 30:21)

The hope of the righteous *shall be gladness*: But the expectation of the wicked shall perish. (Prov. 10:28)

And they, continuing daily with one accord in the temple, and breaking bread from house to house, did eat their meat *with gladness and singleness of heart*. (Acts 2:46)

So we are addressing a biblical concept, but are not using a biblical word for it. Where do we get this word *Chestertonian* for what we are talking about? Chesterton was a character who was renowned for jovial and combative insight. He fought unbelief effectively, but he always fought like a cavalier and never like a thug with a wart on his nose.

And comes now C.S. Lewis describing the early Puritans. I quoted this earlier, but because it is one of my most favorite quotations in the world *ever*, I am going to do it again. If you fail to track with my arguments in this book, I will probably quote it again later.

> But there is no understanding the period of the Reformation in England until we have grasped the fact that the quarrel between the Puritans and the Papists was not primarily a quarrel between rigorism and indulgence, and that, in so far as it was, the rigorism was on the Roman side. On many questions, and specially in their view of the marriage bed, the Puritans were the indulgent party; if we may without disrespect so use the name of a great Roman Catholic, a great writer, and a great man, they were *much more Chestertonian* than their adversaries. (C.S. Lewis, *Selected Literary Essays*, p. 116, emphasis mine)

As participants in a great and true reformation, this attitude really was characteristic of the early Protestants, for the first century or so. Lewis again:

> From this buoyant humility, this farewell to the self with all its good resolutions, anxiety,

scruples, and motive-scratchings, all the
Protestant doctrines originally sprang. (*English Lit*, p. 33)

There were many things going on at that time,
but a driving force in the Reformation was the
free declaration of a free grace that offered free
forgiveness of sin. And the people *knew* it.

And here is the central point—this demeanor,
this Spirit-given, Christ-exalting demeanor—is *an
essential part* of the program. This is not an add-
on extra. This is the beating heart of Calvinism.

And this brings us to a discussion of Trinitarian hedonism. The first thing to note is that John
Piper has done the Church a valuable service
in establishing the inescapability of hedonism
in the well-tempered service of God. The point
is hard for many Christians to swallow, but it is
equally hard to avoid. On this general subject, I
would refer anyone with questions about it to the
basic Piper corpus.

But once we have jackhammered up the
foundation of dour stoicism, and/or anemic pi-
etism, and have poured the foundations of what
it means to seek our true pleasure, we still have
the need to build on that foundation. Here are

a couple blueprint sketches for some areas that still need work.

As Toby Sumpter has pointed out, one of the areas where we need to develop our thinking in this area is by grounding it all in explicitly Trinitarian categories. This should actually be pretty straightforward because all this stuff is in Edwards, and Edwards is *the* American theologian on the Trinity. That's all good, but I leave it to other folks to write *those* books.

In short, it makes a world of difference whether the God who is most glorified by our satisfaction in Him is eternally in relationship with others within the Godhead or not. It means that this hedonism is a hedonism of love, Father, Son, and Spirit, and not a hedonism you might find in a tower of power, as with Allah. So consider *that* to be Hedonism 2.0, Nicaean hedonism.

But then we also need to move on to Chalcedon, to an incarnational hedonism. And this is where we really do need the safety harnesses, and this is where the dour pietists will be warning us with an I-told-you-so censoriousness. Looking ahead, this is where Chesterton is so helpful.

But this is also the place where the dour pietists will sometimes have a point. This is because hedonism makes many people think that we are advancing a frat-boy-party-commando-hedonism, and some will be attracted to *that*, and others will be repulsed by it.

As a consequence, many who are repulsed but who are still compelled to recognize the necessity of self-interest in all creaturely choices, will react into a refined Epicureanism, instead of resorting to the Incarnation. But, at the end of the day, refined hedonism just creates snobs. Sure, they don't find their pleasures in carousing, snorting cocaine, chasing skirts, and whatnot, but rather in taking a stroll through a miniature Japanese garden on a pleasant summer evening, in order to contemplate geometric proofs and chess moves of a higher order. And they are insufferable.

But God made the world, we trashed it, and then the incarnate Christ was born into it in order to redeem the whole thing. He rose from the dead in this world in order to redeem everything about it, beer and bacon included.

So we need to remember the nature of the Creator/creature divide, and how the sovereignty of God determined to cross that divide by means of Jesus the risen Lord. The divide remains what it always was, and the incarnational bridge remains what it always will be, world without end. Now of course this has ramifications for our worship, but it also has ramifications for absolutely everything else.

By the very nature of the case, we cannot present an exhaustive list here, but the ramifications would include beer, mowing the lawn, sex with your wife or husband, brown gravy, sitting on the front porch, listening to a good poem, making movies, getting out the guitar, going to church, and getting a foot rub. There are two sacraments, true, but there is only one sacramental. The *world* is that sacramental, and everything in it. Grace is everywhere and gets into everything. Faith can dig it out of anything. The grandeur of God can flame out from anything, like the shining from shook foil.

If understood, this results in *mediated* grace for everyone who is responding to God in true faith. God does grant immediate grace in various ways, true. When He converts a soul, when He visits someone with direct blessing, when He receives our worship, the grace can be immediate. But this immediate grace is supposed to be a *radiant* grace, spreading out through everything else, affecting everything else, suffusing everything else, causing everything else to become a mirror that reflects the glory of God.

If we don't get this, we will start to think of ourselves as deep-sea divers, who have a grace hose running from our helmet up to Heaven, and the only way we can get grace is down through that hose. But God is the one in whom we live and move and have our being (Acts 17:28). We are living in the presence of God where it is actually possible to offer thanks *for all things* (Eph. 5:20).

Van Til once said that if there were one place on creation's radio dial where nonbelievers could tune in and not hear God, that is where everybody would have their radio set, all the time. His point was of course that God broadcasts, all the time, on every channel. But often, believers make a similar mistake, that of thinking that God broadcasts on only one channel, and then they do their level pious best to keep their radio tuned to that one channel. But then the time comes when the rest of your family and friends tire of hearing the Haven of Rest Quartet 24-7, and so life elsewhere begins to wither and dry up. And sanctifying the rest of the channels does not consist of making them into the same kind of "religious broadcasting."

The problem is that the apostle Paul says that whatever we eat, down to the last French fry, we should do to the glory of God (1 Cor. 10:31). But if we think this means that we need to be sitting in the corner of the fast-food joint, having visions like we were John of Damascus or somebody, we will rapidly become tiresome. More than tiresome. We will become insufferable.

But if we think that the only way to avoid becoming tiresome in this way is by treating the French fry as if it were a neutral, non-combatant in the great spiritual war that swirls around us all, then we are in the process of going over to the other side. We have become compromised.

There is much more to say on this subject, and the Christian Church today desperately needs to hear it. I am fond of saying that dualism is bad juju, and this is yet another manifestation of how it works us over.[1]

We need to act like we have a full tank of gas, and lots of Wyoming ahead. In John Piper's book, *When I Don't Desire God*, there is a chapter entitled "How to Wield the World in the Fight for Joy."

---

1 For those who want to pursue this further (and who doesn't need to?), I would recommend *Notes from the Tilt-a-Whirl* by my son Nate.

And that chapter is filled, of course, with Piper's usual exegetical good sense, along with his careful framing of the question before the house. Having read it, and having agreed with a whole bunch of it, I *still* want to urge us to go further up and further in. Here are a few thoughts on that.

Piper leans on C.S. Lewis' argument in an essay called "Meditation in a Toolshed," which is found in *God in the Dock*. Piper does well in acknowledging that opting out of a bodily recognition of God and His gifts is not actually possible, and the only question is *how* we do it, and not *whether* we do it. He draws on the distinction that Lewis makes between looking *at* something (in this case, a sunbeam), and looking *along* the same beam, back to the sun.

In this chapter, Piper says:

> So the question must be faced: How do we use the created world around us, including our own bodies, to help us fight for joy in God? In God, I say! Not in nature. Not in music. Not in health. Not in food or drink. Not in natural beauty. How can all these good gifts serve joy in God, and not usurp the supreme affections of our hearts? (p. 178)

> Gratitude is *occasioned* by a gift, but is *directed* to the giver. (p. 186)

And this brings us to the real heart of this entire problem—the relationship between Giver and gift. But before addressing this, I want to appear to change the subject for a minute.

I said in the previous section that we needed to work through this in an explicitly Trinitarian way. But this means more than just counting everything we see in groups of three. One of the essential Trinitarian doctrines that we need to apply to this is the doctrine of *perichoresis*, the truth that each member of the Trinity fully indwells each of the others.

For example, Jesus talks about this in the gospel of John:

> Neither pray I for these alone, but for them also which shall believe on me through their word; that they all may be one; as thou, Father, art in me, and I in thee, that they also may be one in us: that the world may believe that thou hast sent me. (John 17:20-21)

Note that the Father indwells the Son completely, and the Son indwells the Father completely.

Notice also that Jesus wants the same kind of thing for us, and so perichoretic indwelling must not be a prerogative of divinity. There is something communicable about it. And so I want to argue that an understanding of perichoretic indwelling helps us to address the vexed question of relating the Giver and His gifts.

Given my finite limitations, I have to think about the gifts God gives to me a *lot*. I have to think about the fact that my feet are not cold anymore, that it is time for dinner, that one of my shoulder blades itches, and so on. To use Lewis' conceit from the toolshed, I have to spend a lot of time looking at the sunbeams, and a fraction of my time is set aside for direct worship of God, looking along the sunbeam. The temptation we have is that of treating all this as a zero-sum game, assuming that any time spent on the gifts is necessarily time away from the Giver.

But though this sometimes happens, it does not need to happen. Rightly handled, a gift is *never* detached from the one who gave it. Wrongly handled, a gift can be the occasion of selfishness, which is a common problem. But it can also be the occasion of a higher form of selfishness,

one which pretends to be above the whole taw-
dry field of "gifts in themselves."

Picture a particularly "pious" little child who
was impossible to give gifts to, because he would
always unwrap it, abandon it immediately, and
run up to his parent and say, "But what really
counts is my relationship with *you!*" A selfish
child playing with a toy ungratefully is forgetting
the giver. But this pious form of purported self-
lessness (but actually selfishness) is refusing to
let the giver even *be* a giver.

We should not assume that in the resurrection,
when we have finally learned how to look along
that beam, in pure worship, that our bodies will
then be superfluous. God will not have given us
eternal and everlasting bodies because we finally got to such a point of spiritual maturity that we
are able to ignore them. In the resurrection, we
will have learned something we currently struggle
with, which is how to live fully integrated lives. If
God is the one in whom we live and move and have
our being, it should not be necessary, in order to
glorify God, to drop everything. We shouldn't have
to keep these things in separate compartments.

Incidentally, this kind of integration will pre-
vent dislocations from arising in families that are

sold out to the glory of God. Integration will keep our neighbor (or wife, or husband, or kids) from feeling like a means to an end. There is a delicate balance here, but God is most glorified in me when I love what He has given to me, *for its own sake*. This is teleologically related to the macro-point of God's glory being over all, of course, but we still have to enjoy what He gives, flat out, period, stop. Otherwise, in the resurrection, God will be looking at all the billions of His resurrected saints, standing there contentedly, looking at Him, and He will say, "You know, you people are impossible to shop for." Which is, of course, absurd and impossible.

In the resurrection, it will be possible for us to be absorbed by God's *gifts* in ways that are impossible to conceive of now.

How might *perichoresis* help us with this? In a perichoretic world, the gift need not displace the Giver, as though they were two billiards balls. In the material world, the space that one object occupies is space that another object cannot occupy. We carry our assumptions about this over into the spiritual world, and we consequently assume that if we are thinking about meat on the grill, bees in the honeysuckle, a sweet wife in bed, beer in a

frosted glass, or a full tank of gas and lots of Wy-
oming ahead, then we cannot be thinking about
God also, or be living in gratitude before Him. But
I don't believe this is the case at all.

When we think about the gifts in exclusion of
the Giver, it is because we are being prideful, or
selfish in some way. If we think about the Giver
only, we are trying hard to be disembodied spir-
its—which is not how the Giver made us, and
if we were paying all that much attention to the
Giver, we ought to have noticed that He didn't
want to make us that way.

If I turn every gift that God gives over in my
hands suspiciously, looking for the idol trap, then I
am not rejoicing before Him the way I ought to be.

So hedonism is not just a "spiritual" thing. We
are forgiven, but remember that we are forgiven
in a material world. But among the pious, the
suspicion that is directed against an exuberant
gratitude for stuff is a suspicion that places the
things of earth in some kind of a competition
with the things of heaven. This world competes
with the eternal things, and so what we think we
must do is get a five-gallon bucket of dour paint
thinner and pour it over all our material posses-
sions. We try to make Heaven thick by making

earth thin. This is wrong-headed and incurs the chastisements of the latter half of Deuteronomy 28 to boot.

What we must do is receive all God's covenant-al blessings, as thick as we can conceive of them, and then imagine how much thicker Heaven will be. *Let Jesus cut the bacon*, in other words.[2]

We receive these blessings, in the name of Christ, as *hors d'oeuvres*, to whet the appetite, to make us long for more. We are not trying to get out of a prison. We are trying to get out of the entry room, and into the mansion.

In George Herbert's lovely poem, *Sunday*, he describes the Lord's Day as "the next world's bud." Later in that same poem, he calls Sunday "a day of mirth." This is no incongruity. James, the Lord's brother, suggested that if someone was *merry*, he should sing psalms (Jas. 5:13).

> Puritan poets . . . knew that part of their work in this world was to wean their affections from the unmixed love of it. But they also knew that this world was God's metaphor for His communicable glories and that

2 For those who want to pursue this, which should be everybody, I would recommend Joe Rigney's book, *The Things of Earth*.

another part of their duty was to see and utter that metaphor, to use the figural value of this world to turn their attentions and affections to the next. (Daly, *God's Altar*, p. 81)

For example, they want to write off all social conservatives as throwback Puritans, with crabbed, pinched faces, worrying desperately that somewhere, somebody called that number on the bathroom wall, and *is* having a good time. The answer is to cultivate a sunny Calvinism, a Chestertonian Calvinism. Chesterton himself would of course be annoyed at my appropriation of his great name to serve as an adjective to my soteriology, but we all have our crosses to bear. (*Rules for Reformers*, p. 53)

That legacy [of C.S. Lewis] is a large contributor to my willingness to luxuriate in my quite oxymoronic goal of becoming and remaining a Chestertonian Calvinist. (From *The Romantic Rationalist*, p. 80)

A Paradox Is Truth Standing on Its Head to Get Attention

T he mind of G.K. Chesterton was a field of ripe corn. Not only was he a prolific source of thoughts, each one a stalk of corn, but each one of them contained hundreds of kernels, each of them capable of multiplying as well. He didn't just write a lot—he was abundantly *fruitful*.

He was at his most fruitful when he talked about the arts and imagination because that is where he happened to be discussing the center of his power as a writer.

In his book on the subject, Chesterton scholar Thomas Peters brings together a delightful set of observations from Chesterton himself on the arts, and then goes on to competently discuss them himself. If you love Chesterton, if you want to write with effect, if you are fond of inexplicable explanations, or all of the above and more, then *The Christian Imagination* is a book you really need to have.

Reading Chesterton is like taking a stroll in the wild, but in an area that is teeming with game. You will see deer, elk, rabbits, and so on. But books of quotations are more like a trip to the zoo—you see more strange animals that way, but they are not in their native habitat, and they are all lined up next to each other. In the case of Chesterton, I recommend both approaches. There is too much to see otherwise.

Gems from Chesterton on the imagination and its failures are found throughout Peters' book. If you are involved in the arena of letters at all, then this book is indispensable. It is probably indispensable regardless. Here is a sample of Chesterton, as quoted by Peters:

> Towers are not tall unless we look up at them; and giants are not giants unless they are larger than we. All this gigantesque imagination, which is, perhaps, the mightiest of the pleasures of man, is at bottom entirely humble. (*The Christian Imagination*, p. 71)

> I am not depreciating telephones; I am complaining that they are not appreciated. I am not attacking inventions; I am attacking indifference to inventions . . . I am not objecting to the statement that the science of the modern world is wonderful; I am only objecting to the modern world because it does not wonder at it. (*TCI*, p. 57)

These citations display the typical Chesterton move, one in which he inverts all the categories, and says the thing directly opposite to what you expected him to say.

On critics, here is Peters summarizing Chesterton.

> Concerning the critics, G.K. had a great deal to say, but his observations can be divided into

> four general issues: their bias against moral-
> ity in the arts, their unreflecting progressiv-
> ism, their incessantly negative orientation,
> and their propensity to faddishness. (p. 71)

Boy, things sure have changed since Chesterton's time!

And the resultant problem with "the critics"
is that they are so entirely pedestrian and predictable. The object of their study, if that object
is Chesterton, is unpredictable—and squirrely.
That is one of the reasons he exasperates them
so much.

Chesterton was quotable above virtually all
men, and one looks in vain for him to handle the
requirements of the footnote-mongers with suf-
ficient gentleness and respect. Chesterton rois-
ters merrily down the highway of thought, with
the more precise-minded following after, picking up after him, correcting a citation here or a
date there. And yet the footnoters highly respect
him (now that he's dead), and will quote him until
the cows find two in the bush, as they say:

> Modesty has moved from the organ of am-
> bition. Modesty has settled upon the organ

> of conviction where it was never meant to
> be. A man was meant to be doubtful about
> himself, but undoubting about the truth:
> this has been exactly reversed. Nowadays
> the part of a man that a man does assert
> is exactly the part he ought not to assert—
> himself. The part he doubts is exactly the
> part he ought not to doubt—the Divine Rea-
> son. (Chesterton, *Orthodoxy*)

There is apparently some debate over whether Chesterton said this next one, but if he didn't, I think we can all agree that he should have, and it was very wrong for him not to have done so.

> When people stop believing in God, they
> don't believe in nothing—they believe in
> anything.

I tried to look up the source for that quote one time, and what I ran into were pages listing "things Chesterton didn't say."

But related to all this, there seems to be an in-verse relationship between the number of foot-notes that Chesterton *uses* and the number of footnotes he is *in*.

This is instructive, and we can look for confirmation at the life of someone who was greatly affected by Chesterton, meaning C.S. Lewis. He was a rare example of someone who could write both ways (using footnotes, as well as being worthy of inclusion in footnotes). Lewis was capable of writing scholarly books that showed a mastery of the literature in his field, and these books (like *The Allegory of Love*, or *English Literature in the Sixteenth Century*) are still valuable as works of scholarship today. But he wrote another

way as well, in Chesterton's way, with virtually no footnotes or scholarly apparatus. These are the books by which he is chiefly remembered, and they too, like Chesterton's works, will show up in footnotes and bibliographies for the next five hundred years or so.

Chesterton knew that loving and fighting go together.

> To love a thing without wishing to fight for it is not love at all; it is lust.

> He knows that loving the world is the same thing as fighting the world. (*Appreciation and Criticism of the Works of Charles Dickens*)

Chesterton rejects the silliness of today's philosophers who want to separate loving and fighting, putting them into separate camps. This is well represented by the glib placard of the sixties, urging us to make love, not war.

This false juxtaposition is trying to hide the fact that *it is always both*. Either you make love indiscriminately, and make war on the resultant offspring, or you make love to one woman for life and fight to protect her and the children you have fathered. If you determine that it is too militant to fight in the latter way, then the love you have chosen in the former way is simply lust, a lust that reduces to war on the unborn.

We can see that this is how it is unfolding in the West today. Lunatic wars and lunatic lusts go together. So do chivalric wars and chivalric romances. The pacifist who doesn't want to fight the dragon for the sake of the lady is actually in the process of becoming a dragon himself. This reality is sometimes obscured by the missing nostril flame and hidden claws, but there is a ready explanation. Pacifists are just passive-aggressive dragons.

We have gotten to that stage in the battle where the forces have fully joined, and there is no longer—properly speaking—a front. We do not have a distinguishable *line* anymore. It is more like a melee, with different colored uniforms everywhere. And this is why every topic has been swept up into the conflict. What we need is clear thinking in the melee, and there is no one like Chesterton to help us.

Where can you go where the ruling elites will agree to leave you alone? Can you change a light bulb? Can you fry up some bacon? Can you decline joining in the mandatory celebrations of a same-sex mirage? Can you keep your doctor? Are you allowed to use plastic bags?

Chesterton said somewhere that our task is to fly the flag of the world—and we should know that this is something that is certain to bring us into conflict with the world. We affirm a fundamental creational loyalty to the world, and constantly thwart the world's desire to become disloyal to itself. This is why it is good to be earthy, and bad to be worldly.

Worldliness is just a clever way of deserting the world, and to "get" that is to understand how Chesterton thinks. Feminism is simply a way of despising femininity. Staring at your iPhone all day is failing to be amazed at it.

This is why a battle in a philosophy class over the correspondence view of truth is connected to the marriage debates, which in turn is connected to the environment, which in turn is connected to just-war theory, which in turn is connected to the correspondence view of truth.

Everything is connected. Everything matters. Nonsense tolerated anywhere will metastasize, and the results are always ugly.

> When the people have got used to unreason
> they can no longer be startled at injustice.

In the broken windows theory of law enforcement, disregard of the law in petty things signals an unwillingness to deal with anything, and so the situation rapidly deteriorates. Some broken windows tolerated will lead to many more broken windows, and it gets worse from there.

It is the same kind of thing with nonsense. When we refuse to police the boundaries between sense and nonsense in our daily affairs, it is not long before that boundary is ignored everywhere. This is just another instance of the centrality of peripherals.

And by "centrality of peripherals" I do not mean to veer into a form of Zen Presbyterianism.

This does not mean favoring the peripherals *instead* of the center. That would be the sin of majoring on minors, swallowing camels, and all the rest of it. But remember, the fruit—which Christ required for identifying the nature of a tree—is way out on the edges of the tree and is at the farthest point away from the root. We must recover the understanding that peripherals are central because the center is important.

This is one of the reasons why Chesterton is so good in discussing the ordinary issues of life. He can pluck any fruit from any branch and, without changing the subject, trace the life of that fruit back to the root. Take manners, for example. Manners can be described as love in trifles, love at the periphery. The collapse of manners in our society—a peripheral thing, surely!—represents a true downgrade. But here is Chesterton:

> Love of humanity is the commonest and most natural of the feelings of a fresh nature, and almost everyone has felt it alight capriciously upon him when looking at a crowded park or on a room full of dancers.

Those activities are out at the edges, but *by looking at the edges we can see the center.* You give the last piece of pie to God, who doesn't eat pie, by giving it to your neighbor, who does. That is the point of courtesy, manners, etiquette— consider 1 Pet. 2:17; 3:7; 1 Tim. 5:17; 6:1; Eph. 6:2; Rom. 12:10; 13:7.

Another example of the same kind of thing is found in the realm of aesthetics. Relativism has compromised us here as nowhere else. A clear-headed man will want to say that some music, paintings, sculpture, etc. are just plain dumb and stupid. But we immediately hear the retort—"who is to say . . .?" Our inability to identify rotten fruit on the branches means that we are especially unable to identify a problem at the root.

> There must always be a rich moral soil for any great aesthetic growth. The principle of art for art's sake is a very good principle if it means that there is a vital distinction between the earth and the tree that has its root in the earth; but it is a very bad principle if it means that the tree could grow just as well with its roots in the air.

This applies to absolutely everything. Let the reader understand.

Why Chesterton Wouldn't Fit in Skinny Jeans

O ne time I was reviewing a book called *The Truth About Organic Foods*, and I had occasion to quote Chesterton. This raised an important question in the minds of some—where do I get off quoting Chesterton in the midst of a post that, for all intents and purposes, looked to some like a valiant attempt to keep my Monsanto stock from collapsing completely? It didn't look that way to others, like to *me*, but let's leave that to the side for a moment, and simply address the Chesterton question.

Chesterton was the genuine article, and the contemporary organic foods movement (and every associated form of hipsterism) isn't. He wore an artificial and manufactured cape to cover a heart that did nothing but overflow with authentic Christian insight. This, as opposed to those who wear a Central American coarse-woven authenticity cape to cover up the aching hollowness within. There is a difference, as he might say, between a man who stands in the face of all the prevailing winds, and the one who is driven before all the prevailing winds. There is a distinct difference between the convex and concave sides of the sail.

And as soon as we have grasped the difference, we will have also grasped that the difference is *not a subtle one*.

Chesterton had no use for cant or for the *poseurs* who deliver it. But you don't identify the *poseur* by which pose he is copping, but rather by the participle, by the act of posing itself. A poseur can be smiling or glowering for any number of cameras. He might be a New Testament scholar, a gym rat, a hipster, a poet, or a smooth ladies' man. He might be any number of things. We do not identify him by the costume he is wearing, but rather by the fact that he always has one eye on the lookout for a camera or a mirror.

The contemporary hipster is a recent phenomenon (in terms of what we used to call in the Navy the uniform-of-the-day), but the broader category of hipster has been with us since at least the time of Rousseau. The *type* was well-known to Chesterton, and, had there been a Whole Foods in Victorian London, we would have had some choice epigrams from Chesterton on the kind of poet who made a point of shopping for exotic cheeses there.

In fact, here is one, written long before the word *metrosexual* was even coined.

> The old artist remained proud in spite of his unpopularity; the new artist is proud because of his unpopularity; perhaps it is his chief ground for pride.

And if you can't find an outlet to plug this into, then you clearly have the wrong kind of adapter.

Chesterton would never, ever cop a pose because he thought it was ironic and clever—although he would grant that he had ordinary human vanity and say that he thought it ironic and clever because he had copped it. He adopted an offbeat *persona*, which some thought of as eccentric, but the category of eccentricity is not the same thing as the category of *conformist* eccentricity.

Once as a boy I was improving my mind by reading *Mad* magazine, and I came across an epigram from Alfred E. Newman, which has helped to shape my entire outlook on these matters. He said, "Today's non-conformists are getting harder and harder to tell apart." Quite distinct from this, when Chesterton took his stand, it was a brilliant one, and *sui generis*. He was one of a kind.

Today's rebellions are all commodified. If the rebels of next week start wearing whatever the anti-consumerist uniform is, you can be pretty sure that the decision about what was going to be hot was made in a board room somewhere in Manhattan, a board room with a big mahogany table. People wear *Stick It to the Man* t-shirts because the Man told them to.

That this is the ironic-and-non-self-aware assumption of today's rebels can be seen at a glance. How else would it be possible for a generation of young people to adopt the worldview and outlook of the ruling elites, all the major corporations, virtually every university on the continent, all the major media outlets, the top brass at the Pentagon, and still have the unvarnished nerve to think of themselves as the *resistance*.

Every generation has its hypocrisies, and this results in certain rascals pretending to have attained to the highest virtue recognized by that generation. Unfortunately, our highest virtue is authenticity, not-being-fake, being non-hypocritical. So that is what this hypocritical generation is pretending to be. They are all pretending to not be hypocrites, and they are doing it hypocritically. As Sam Goldwyn once said, "The secret of success is sincerity. Once you can fake that you've got it made."

The difference between Chesterton and the modern *poseurs* is that he was the real thing, and they are not. Moreover, they are being inauthentic about authenticity.

Chesterton once said that fallacies do not cease to be fallacies simply because they have become fashions, and who better to take this warning to heart than that contemporary class of person for whom virtually *all* intellectual energy is devoted to staying fashionable?

Of course Chesterton loved paradox—he said that a paradox was truth standing on its head to get attention—but he knew the difference between paradox and simple confusion and contradiction.

Throughout his body of work, again and again, he demolishes the contradictions of pretension and builds lasting monuments to true Christian irony.

One of our current confusions (which Chesterton is not here to address, unfortunately), and which his heirs must therefore take up in their own inadequate fashion, is what to say about a movement whose two patron saints are apparently Wendell Berry and Steve Jobs.

Chesterton summed it up this way:

> Oscar Wilde said that sunsets were not valued because we could not pay for sunsets. But Oscar Wilde was wrong; we can pay for sunsets. We can pay for them by not being Oscar Wilde.

And by not being his descendants.

A Most Reasonable
Reticence

One of the ways that Chesterton is so helpful is that he puts the common back into common sense. He is a staunch defender of God's created moral order, but at the same time, he understands—as few others have done—that there is a stark difference between morality and being fastidious. There were a number of times where the prophets of God came out of the wilderness in order to uphold the holiness of the law, but they did so using language that struck the pious Jews of their day like paint thinner on a paper cut. But . . .

> Nine times out of ten it is the coarse word that condemns an evil, and the refined word that excuses it. (Chesterton)

The way I seek to operate in this cloistered fundamentalist world of mine is quite different than sometimes appears in my public writing. My daily conversation and manner of life is rated a squeaky-clean G. But—you may have noticed—my blog is sometimes PG-13, or, depending on how sequestered you are, sometimes R.

I largely live in a Christian subculture that prizes public and defined reticence on certain topics, modesty and decorum from our womenfolk, decorum and manners from our menfolk, and certain topics being just plain off limits for the sake of decency and good taste. I *like* it that we live like that, and I want to do everything in my power to preserve the high tone and teach others what it is like to live this way.

Some might call it a bubble, but I would actually compare it to a haven carved out of a wilderness. Let's just call it Sherwood Forest. It is a profanity-free land of Goshen, while the rest of Egypt is being pelted with f-bombs.

My standards for public life between the sexes come out of the world made famous by Mike Pence, and not the world made infamous by Harvey Weinstein. And it would be nice if we could remember the brutal treatment of Pence at the hands of all the cool kids when it was discovered that he conducted himself such that he could not plausibly be accused of certain kinds of vile behavior. We are talking about the kind of behavior that apparently was an "open secret" in the kind of places that the cool kids (who mocked Pence) were accustomed to inhabit.

So *fight* for your right to live with your people in a way that honors decency, and that gives such decency an environment in which it can thrive. That means manners, it means chivalry, and it means a defined standard of decency. It means reticence. And it therefore means resorting to Chesterton often. But Chesterton is moral, not dainty.

This also means recognizing that men and women are different clean down to the bone. It means realizing that those differences are relevant in every field of human endeavor. The headship of the husband is relevant in more places than in breaking the tie vote between husband and wife. It is important in more areas than in just prohibiting women from pulpit ministry. Men and women are different *everywhere*. Common sense, man.

But an important part of this fight means speaking outside (to the world) in a way that you do not ever do inside. You wield your sword on the battlefield, and not in your living room. When it comes to fighting those whose agenda for our culture *is fundamentally indecent*, it is crucial that we do not fall for their old euphemism ploy.

So here is Chesterton, on point as usual:

> When somebody wishes to wage a social war against what all normal people have regarded as a social decency, the very first thing he does is to find some artificial term that shall sound relatively decent.

Marriage equality sounds so much better than solemnized sodomy. Chesterton calls this sort of thing "publicity experts picking pleasant expressions for unpleasant things; and I for one prefer the coarse language of our fathers" (Chesterton, *On Evil Euphemisms*). And as he notes above, the blunt term is usually the honest one, while the effete term is a dainty cover for corruption.

Whenever we have any sense that this is happening around us, our first duty and responsibility is to put our foot clean through the side of it.

In the aftermath of the Weinstein fireball, any number of actresses came forward to tell their stories, detailing the ways in which the former movie mogul tried to see them in the nude. This was silly of him, because all he needed to do is watch them in one of his own movies.

What I am arguing for I will say yet again. *You can't have it both ways.* You cannot establish a culture that has institutionalized the abandonment of the unique dignity of women, and then, when the culture starts acting on that perverse premise, suddenly find some dignity for them to stand on. You don't have any of that dignity anymore. You threw it *away*, remember?

And you mercilessly mocked those who objected to throwing it away. You laughed at their predictions.

They objected to discarding a unique feminine dignity, and you mocked them. When the consequences of having lost that dignity start to manifest themselves—as they will continue to do with increasing regularity—you hate and despise them. You hate them for being right in the prediction, and you hate them because their "misogynist" subcultures are among the few remaining places where women are not treated like that.

Everything these vile people have been saying, doing, teaching, touching, filming, and litigating, for the last 40 years, *has been a lie*. People are starting to notice it.

Chesterton again, speaking through Father Brown:

> The first effect of not believing in God, is
> that you lose your common sense.

Common sense is not limited to things like closing the window when the living room gets chilly. Common sense includes, right at the center, a moral sense. And it knows enough to distinguish manners from morals.

My Favorite Papist

When it comes to getting RSVPs back for all the invitations we sent out to the Chesterton Appreciation Party, at least from the conservative Protestants we invited, we have noticed a certain reluctance. This is due to the simple fact that Chesterton was a Roman Catholic. Moreover, it has to be said that he was, um, somewhat of an exuberant one. I mean, he thought that Thomas Aquinas levitated once.

Other Protestants might repine a little, saying that they mostly appreciate his book *Orthodoxy*,

which was written while he was still an Anglican. Still other Protestants have bought into the
lowest common denominator version of ecume-
nicity, so they are prepared to just ignore the differences between Rome and Geneva, beaming
an ecumenical smile as they do so. But this still
leaves the convinced and confessional Protestants somewhat conflicted. They are Bible believers, and hence they are the ones most attracted
to Chesterton's ability to simply demolish secularist nonsense, and at the same time they are
the ones most likely to be peeved and annoyed
when Chesterton turns his sixteen-inch guns of
wit, drollery, and repartee on *them*.

And so when this happens, the central stum-
bling block is Chesterton's embrace of the Roman
system, all the way out on the skinny branches.
What are we to make of this? How could Chesterton be so *wise* on so many things, and miss
things so completely when it comes to this issue? It is kind of like watching Babe Ruth strike
out six times in a row. Nobody likes it when that
scenario happens, and they start thinking about
heading for the parking lot.

Allow me to propose a model for processing
this. As we imitate Chesterton, we may learn from

him a model for debating in a Chestertonian way, including those times when we find ourselves debating Chesterton himself. Chesterton once showed us the way. As noted earlier, Chesterton once said, "Oscar Wilde said that sunsets were not valued because we could not pay for sunsets. But Oscar Wilde was wrong; we can pay for sunsets. We can pay for them by not being Oscar Wilde." In a similar way, we can be Chestertonian on the gospel by not being Chesterton.

We should begin by noting the difference between the objective facts of the gospel—the death, burial, and resurrection of Christ—and the subjective response to the gospel—repentance and belief.

Now when it comes to the former, there is no difference between classical Protestantism and the Roman church. Both affirm that Christ died, was buried, and rose. We agree on the facts of history. The corruptions and mistakes of Rome are introduced later in the story, with their explanations of how the grace resident in that historical moment is applied to the individual sinner. They believe that the repentance and belief that are needed are supplied by the person being saved, and that the grace that he needs in order to do this is mediated to him through an authorized representative of the Church, who is trained to oversee the apparatus of salvation—which in this case are the seven sacraments.

In this view, the grace of God is contained in a vast reservoir, and there are seven gold-plated spigots from which that grace is dispensed, and these spigots are manned by ordained priests. Now to be fair, this is *structurally* identical to how much of pop evangelicalism operates—only they dispense the grace through undecorated tin buckets and green garden hoses—meaning altar calls, signing cards, throwing pinecones in the fire at youth camp, re-dedications, and all the rest of it. The semi-Pelagianism of Rome is more than matched by the semi-Pelagianism of a Billy Graham crusade.

But in classical Protestant theology, the grace of God is not like a reservoir at all, maintained by ecclesiastical functionaries, but is more like a tsunami, coming in from the infinite oceans of grace. We have no control over it whatsoever.

The power that accomplishes this salvation is resident in the objective gospel, and however much religious professionals try to stage-manage the tsunami, it always flows into places that

officious priests and parsons did not give it per-
mission to go. He is not a tame lion. Because He
is not a tame lion, we have to reckon with the fact
that He is always consistent, never predictable.
Semper constans, numquam praedici.

For example, how many of us have read the
story of the Pharisee and the tax collector going
down to the Temple to pray, and have observed
with disgust the Pharisee thanking God that he
was not like that tax collector over there (Luke 18:
9-14), and then gone home thanking God that we
were not like that Pharisee?

Now Chesterton is someone who affirms the
objective facts of the gospel, which is good. And
to a certain extent, he also gets the nature of this
tsunami, but also (for reasons of high romance)
wants to remain loyal to the priests guarding the
gold-plated spigots. He hates the prigs and the
prudes who get self-righteous about *anything*,
including Protestant prigs who despised the dec-
orations in the name of despising the doctrine.

> It is always simple to fall; there are an in-
> finity of angles at which one falls, only one
> at which one stands. To have fallen into
> any one of the fads from Gnosticism to

> Christian Science would indeed have been
> obvious and tame. But to have avoided
> them all has been one whirling adventure;
> and in my vision the heavenly chariot flies
> thundering through the ages, the dull here-
> sies sprawling and prostrate, the wild truth
> reeling but erect. (Chesterton, *Orthodoxy*)

On this point, Chesterton is like Plato in the story of one of his exchanges with Diogenes the Cynic. One time Diogenes came to Plato's house and wiped his feet ostentatiously on the ornate rug. "Thus I trample on the pride of Plato," he said. "With greater pride," Plato said mildly.

Chesterton gets the fact that real salvation is wild. This leads him to defend things that are not wild at all. Because of the freedom and grace that dominated his heart, he tended to *project*, assuming that ignorant medieval priests and monks understood grace the same way he did. The fact that they by and large didn't scarcely slows Chesterton down. He covers over their failures with gaudy metaphors. And given a choice between taking a swing at some Puritan Pecksniff or some monkish gnat strangler, he always goes after the Protestant. This is a serious and glaring fault in

Chesterton. It is a good thing we are not saved by good works.

So the fact that classical Protestants regard his Catholicism as a real blind spot in Chesterton should not make us assume that he has blind spots everywhere. Perhaps we might even allow that he might be able to see certain things where *we* have blind spots. Us? Blind spots? Heaven forfend.

But this brings us to the central objection. Surely we can't just dismiss blind spots if they are blind spots with regard to the *gospel*, right? Because I have said publicly before that I believe that Chesterton was saved, I have periodically been assailed for tampering with the gospel, as though I approved of his errors. If Rome is wrong on the gospel, and Chesterton stands with Rome, then that makes him wrong on the gospel—and that makes him a false teacher, one that we shouldn't be emulating. But if the structural (and very serious) error of semi-Pelagianism requires us to say that no one ever got saved through the ministry of such churches or persons, then that would require us to say that nobody ever got right with God at a Billy Graham crusade, which is absurd.

I grant that we should not be following Chesterton's teaching on the relationship of grace and faith, and the nature of the new birth. He was wrong, and the classical Protestants are right. So why do I believe that he could be saved then? Well, because he was wrong, and the classical Protestants are right.

It goes like this. Protestants believe that we are saved by grace, through faith, apart from works of the law. The works that do *not* contribute to our salvation in any way are ceremonial, moral, liturgical, or doctrinal. We are not saved by big works, and we are not saved by tiny works. Neither are we saved by scoring 100% on the soteriology portion of any theology exam. We are saved by the grace of God—which always goes wherever it wants—plus nothing else.

Now if Rome were correct, and we could sin our way out of the grace of God, then the papists are in real trouble. They pray to *pictures*, man.

So a man is not justified through being correct in his doctrine of justification. To maintain that would be a *denial* of the doctrine of justification. I compare it to the difference between the electrician that you hire to wire your house, and the two-year-old who knows how to turn on the lights. If the ordained electricians are not grilled at presbytery about the proper way to wire houses, then they are going to have a ministry that is the cause of many unfortunate house fires. You want the presbytery exam to be thorough in its schematic testing of the man's understanding of the *ordo salutis*. But the two-year-old might have many erroneous conceptions about what happens whenever he flips the switch, and yet those erroneous conceptions do not keep the room dark.

The room lights up despite those erroneous conceptions precisely *because* we are saved by grace, not by works. And conversely, a trained electrician might be absolutely correct in his description of how the circuits are supposed to go, but because of some inner mystery of lawlessness, be living in the dark himself.

John Newton described this problem well.

> Whatever it be that makes us trust in ourselves that we are comparatively wise or good, so as to treat those with contempt who do not subscribe to our doctrines, or follow our party, is a proof and fruit of a self-righteous spirit. Self-righteousness can feed

upon doctrines, as well as upon works; and a
man may have the heart of a Pharisee, while
his head is stored with orthodox notions of
the unworthiness of the creature and the
riches of free grace.

In short, Calvinists know that there is nothing
to boast of in man, but some fall into the trap of
boasting in *that* knowledge. They take pride in
knowing that there is nothing to take pride in.

And so, to round out the illustration, I would
not trust Chesterton to wire a house for me. At
the same time, I recognize that he did live in a
room that was well lit, and that in that well lit
room he could observe many things that are of
great benefit to the rest of us. And I would also
add that the Lord has used him to humble the
pride of a number of orthodox electricians.

Gospel Inversions

The world is a sinful place, which means that the ordinary way of looking at things is quite possibly the wrong way. The world is cock-eyed, which means that right-side up might actually be up-side down. And yet, when someone like Chesterton points this out, there is frequently the satisfying sound of hearing a click from the seat belt of common sense.

Pessimism is not in being tired of evil but in being tired of good. Despair does not lie in

> being weary of suffering, but in being weary
> of joy. It is when for some reason or other
> the good things in a society no longer work
> that the society begins to decline; when its
> food does not feed, when its cures do not
> cure, when its blessings refuse to bless.
> (Chesterton, *The Everlasting Man*, p. 153)

Rene Girard calls this social condition that Chesterton is describing a time of sacrificial crisis. Nothing coheres, nothing hangs together, nothing *tastes*.

One of the reasons societies in this condition (as *we* currently very much are) start to disintegrate is related to this. While drumbeat demands for deeper and greater sacrifice come more rapidly, and are insistently louder, the law of diminishing returns has kicked in. Each new huge effort to get the bottle top off reveals to us that we have merely opened one more bottle of lame sauce—and we already had a row of them opened and lined up on the counter.

> We have been with child, we have been
> in pain, We have as it were brought forth
> wind; We have not wrought any deliverance

in the earth; Neither have the inhabitants of
the world fallen. (Isaiah 26:18)

And with each new crisis, the resultant hue
and cry that is set up, in which there are calls for
shared sacrifice, or increased sacrifice, or deeper sacrifice, is a cry that is lifted up by someone
clever enough to want to get out in front of the
mob. When crowds are calling for sacrifice, you
can depend upon it, they are looking for the sacrifice of somebody *else*. Get in the right position
early, man.

And this is why, for Christians, all coercion
should be such a big deal. Simple coercion, absent direct instruction from Scripture, is a big
sin, and manipulative coercion, absent clear instruction from Scripture, is also a big sin. The
way of vicarious substitution, which is what Jesus did on the cross, is *how* He overthrew all such
coercive principalities and powers. Their way is
doomed forever, and the sooner Christians learn
to be done with it the better.

But the carnal heart turns naturally to making
other people do things. When this kind of thing
was going on, Chesterton could identify it in a
glance, and demolish it with a throwaway line.

This is why we must see the levy, or the referendum, or the law, or the conscription *for whatever it is*, and we must then follow it all the way out to the end of the process. When you don't do what they say, men with guns show up at your house.

Now this is quite proper when it is the house of a murderer, or rapist, or an IRS man from Cincinnati. But suppose it is just a regular guy trying to make a living who had a duck land in a puddle enough times for his land to be declared a wetland by the EPA? They still show up with the guns.

This conclusion has to be developed more, but this is why the substitutionary atonement of Jesus Christ is so important. If Christ died in our place, then this central fact of human history is sheer gift. If we follow the folly of Abelard and say that the death of Christ was *mere* example, what we have is a way of the cross with no power of grace. And when sheer grace is not center stage, coercion is always there, standing in the wings.

This is not to deny that Christ died as an example—the apostle Peter absolutely affirms this (1 Pet. 2:21). But I said *mere* example. Do you see? If Christ died as a substitute, *that* is our example to follow. If He did not, *then it isn't*. This why Paul tells husbands to love their wives as Christ loved the church and gave Himself up for her. Without this glorious principle of substitution, the way of the cross always turns into scolding and hectoring people—and the end of that story is always men with guns.

With this said, we have to understand that there are two kinds of substitution. If we superimpose one of them on the gospel story, the grotesque message that results is appalling. If we read the story with the other one in mind, then everything falls into place.

The first kind of substitution is the kind of thing you see in a basketball game. The coach pulls one player, and puts another one in. One comes out, and another goes in. The second kind of substitution is what happens with representation. The people in a district elect a particular representative and he goes to Congress. When he votes, the people vote. When he is courageous, the people are proud. When he is caught up in a scandal, the people are humiliated.

Now look what happens when you try to apply the first kind of substitution to the story of the death of Jesus. We were sinful, and God was mad about it, and apparently needed to kill *somebody*. For some reason, He settled on Jesus, and so Jesus died so that we might live. But what kind of a wicked judge would go for something like that? An evil twin is about to be sentenced to death, and his good twin stands up in the courtroom and offers to take his brother's place. Apart from the noble intentions of the good twin, what kind of a *judge* would say, "Hey, that sounds like a good idea . . ."?

The Lord died as a representative, covenant substitute. Jesus represented us into a holy condition in exactly the same way that Adam represented us into a sinful condition. Adam disobeyed for us *at* a tree; the Lord Jesus obeyed for us *on* a tree. And the latter is no more a legal fiction than the former was.

So we should want the men who come to your house to have no message of coercion or perpetual violence at all. We should want them to be men with good news about this latter kind of staggering substitution, a message about the final violence. And they should have lives that match.

The Greatest Joke

M alcolm Muggeridge was a true kindred spirit to Chesterton, and in more ways than one. He was born just 29 years after Chesterton, so their lives overlapped a bit. Another area where they overlapped was in their view of evolution. Muggeridge once said this about how evolution will fare in retrospect:

> I myself am convinced that the theory of evolution, especially to the extent to which it has been applied, will be one of the

greatest jokes in the history books of the future. Posterity will marvel that so very flim-
sy and dubious an hypothesis could be accepted with the incredible credulity it has.

Muggeridge and Chesterton both had highly
developed senses of humor, and thus they both
recognized a great joke when they saw one. They
were also thinkers who could see to the root of
a matter, and thus both had grown increasingly
dubious about evolution as they matured. The
same thing happened to C.S. Lewis—he began by
accepting evolution as a tenable method for God
to use in creating us, as can be seen in his early
book *The Problem of Pain*, but as he grew older,
he started to think the claims of Darwin to be
radically dangerous. Lewis was friends with an
ardent creationist named Bernard Acworth, and
in 1951, Lewis wrote this in a letter to Acworth:

> I must confess it has shaken me: not in
> my belief in evolution, which was of the
> vaguest and most intermittent kind, but
> in my belief that the question was wholly
> unimportant. I wish I were younger. What
> inclines me now to think that you may be

> right in regarding it as the central and rad-
> ical lie in the whole web of falsehood that
> now governs our lives is not so much your
> arguments against it as the fanatical and
> twisted attitudes of its defenders.

And by 1954, Lewis had written a poem entitled *Evolutionary Hymn*, which is, shall we say,
insufficiently reverent.

> Lead us, Evolution, lead us
> Up the future's endless stair;
> Chop us, change us, prod us, weed us.
> For stagnation is despair:
> Groping, guessing, yet progressing,
> Lead us nobody knows where.

In this attitude, Muggeridge and Lewis had a
great deal in common with Chesterton, who was
directing his hoots at Darwin quite a bit earlier. Remember that Chesterton was born just 15
years after Darwin first published *Origin*, and
the whole thing was still pretty fresh. We are
dealing with Darwinism in its senescence and
have something of an advantage, while Chesterton could see how bad it was in its prime.

> Darwinism was a failure as a true philoso-
> phy; but it was a success as a false religion.
> (MQC, p. 118)

> Darwinism became a fashion long before any-
> body really thought it was a fact. (MQC, 118)

> The sea, out of which all organic life origi-
> nally came: so at least I am informed by the
> "Outline of History," and other fairy-tales of
> science. (*More Quotable Chesterton*, p. 166)

Now this marvelous fact about Chesterton is actually a source of distress to the very capable Chesterton scholar, Ralph Wood. Wood points out that Chesterton took a very dim view of evolution, doing so increasingly so as his life went on. The quotes above really do fairly represent Chesterton's plain dismissal of Darwin.

> As a result, Chesterton came to an almost
> wholly negative estimate of Darwin's dis-
> coveries and theories. (p. 16)

> The later Chesterton becomes almost ob-
> sessed instead, with exorcizing the devil

> of evolution . . . He thus approaches some-
> thing akin to modern theories of 'intelligent
> design' that deny the presence of chance in
> the natural order. (p. 21)

But the odd thing here is that Wood, far from thinking this yet one more feather in the greatly festooned Chestertonian cap, treats it as a fault, as a blemish in the life of his hero.

> His treatment of the vexed question of evo-
> lution is shaky indeed . . . (p. 16).

But Chesterton's take on Darwin is far from shaky, and Wood's critique of him results in a jumbled confusion of nature/grace distinctions. Wood, like N.T. Wright on the same topic, wants to move the discussion of whether God created the world from one branch of theology, where it belongs, to another one, where it doesn't. Wright wants to consider strict creationists as gnostics, which is very similar to Wood's concerns. More about all this in a minute.

There are two broad approaches to the question of God's creation of all things. I am talking here about the divergent views taken by Christian theists. One wants the *ex-nihilo* creation of all matter, energy, and time to be long, long ago, and very far away. Put in that position, we don't have to think about it very much, and we can shroud the whole thing in mysteries that we don't have to answer any questions about. The other view, the one that I am stoutly comfortable with, might be called the *blammo* view of creation. About ten thousand years ago, as the crow flies, there was nothing, and absolutely nothing underneath, above, or around that nothing. And then about four thousand years after that, also as the crow flies, God said, "Let there be light," and *blammo*, there it was.

This is an in-your-face kind of creation. God made the world the same way an artisan fashions things on a workbench in front of him. It is not layered in metaphors or learned distinctions or literary devices. God made Adam out of *dirt*, and He made Eve out of Adam's *rib*. And when God presented the woman to the man, and he asked where she came from, her reply was not "from my pre-Adamite hominoid ancestors."

Now Wood wants this kind of thinking to be considered a failure to maintain the right kind of nature/grace distinction. In other words, he wants to identify the current scientific consensus *about* nature with nature itself. And it is quite true that if currently accepted wild scientific speculations about nature are to be identified with nature itself, then to deny those speculations would be to deny nature.

But how does that make sense? What we are talking about are the divergent views of how the undisputed *nature* got here. Let's make Eve a stand-in for all of nature. If Adam thought she was taken from his side, and he was still sore in fact, and a scientific Johnny in a white lab coat showed up to maintain that, to the contrary, she came from the pre-Adamite hominoids, then what? Neither version of Eve is any the less natural. The fact that nature was created somewhat abruptly does not in the slightest make it any less natural.

When Jesus turned the water into wine at Cana, the resultant wine was true wine. It was a supernatural act that brought it into being suddenly, but the wine itself was as natural as the wine that had already been drunk. And because it was better wine, we cannot say that it was unnatural in any way.

Wood even goes so far as to complain that a self-evident truth like irreducible complexity is somehow a problem.

Even such a notion as "irreducible complexity" holds Christianity hostage to science. (p. 25)

But no. It doesn't make Christianity hostage to
science. It makes the affirmations of the Christian faith consonant with the affirmations of
plain reason. Someone who knows what irreducible complexity is can look at an intricately designed mechanism in nature and say, "This could
not have happened by itself." How is it a threat to
the Christian faith to look at the entire cosmos
and say, "This could not have happened by itself."

And how could the idea of intelligent design
present any kind of threat to those of us who believe that God designed absolutely everything,
and that He is infinitely intelligent?

In order to reason correctly about the world
around us, we need a firm place to stand. That
place is what God has revealed about Himself in
His Word, what He has revealed about Himself in
the created order, and what He has revealed about
Himself in the human conscience, with all of it
being read by reason that has been illuminated by
the Spirit of God. And this divinely taught reason
is something that does not evolve at all.

He cannot tell whether he ought to evolve
into the higher morality or into the larger
morality, unless he has some principle of
pity or of liberty that does not evolve at all.
(*More Quotable Chesterton*, p. 167)

In Praise of Bunyan

Chesterton was at heart a journalist, so the topics he addressed, and the way he addressed them, were all over the road. As something of a tribute, then, as we have begun to think about bringing our study to a close, we too will be all over the road.

Consider this chapter as something of a miscellany, a hodge-podge, an assortment, a gallimaufry, a salmagundi. You know, one of those. Being found in a book that is also like that, it fits right in.

We may begin by noting that Chesterton was a fair-minded bigot. We have before acknowledged that Chesterton was the very opposite of a Calvinism fan, and he did this while not knowing very much about it. At the same time, even though he took such a dim view of Puritans as a class, he could be genuinely magnanimous about some of them—despite his general distaste of Calvinism. Let me give a few examples in some comments he made about Bunyan, a quintessential Calvinist.

Bear constantly in mind that these comments were not proceeding from any deep affection that Chesterton had for the Puritans. Chesterton was a big man, and consequently had some really big blind spots. But Bunyan's ability to *write* was certainly not in that blind spot.

> *The Pilgrim's Progress* certainly exhibits all the marks of such a revival of primitive power and mystery . . . Nowhere, perhaps except in Homer, is there such a perfect description conveyed by the use of merely plain words. (p. 205)

Except in *Homer*?

Neither was the Puritan aptitude for fighting in his blind spot. Chesterton was willing to take his hat off in recognition of Cromwell's great abilities also. Bunyan served a stint in the Parliamentary Army under Cromwell, and Chesterton puts Bunyan and Cromwell side by side as great men.

> Before the Puritans were swept off the scene for ever, they had done two extraordinary things. They had broken to pieces in plain battle on an English meadow the chivalry of a great nation, bred from its youth to arms. And they had brought forth from the agony a small book, called *The Pilgrim's Progress*, which was greater literature than the whole contemporary culture of the great Renaissance, founded on three generations of the worship of learning and art. (p. 206)

These were not things said in a fit of absent-mindedness. Chesterton makes the same point again elsewhere. Once we see Chesterton's willingness to tip his hat to the "discipline of the new army, and the patience and genius of Cromwell" (*A Short History of England*, p. 132), we can note his baseline fair-mindedness. Cromwell and Chesterton were not exactly working on the same project together, at least not knowingly, and yet Chesterton is more than willing to pay tribute to Cromwell's very obvious abilities.

And returning to Bunyan, in another example of this same kind of thing, Chesterton's admiration for John Bunyan has to be right up near the ceiling.

> One of the very greatest and most human geniuses of the not very human seventeenth century was John Bunyan. His work is rightly regarded as a model and monument of completed English. (*Short History*)

Referring to a passage where Chesterton was talking about Bunyan and de Balzac and Dante all together, Kevin Belmonte makes this very apt observation:

> This was rare and celebrated company. Clearly, as a literary critic, Chesterton wished to render good service to Bunyan— who'd taught him things worth keeping. (Kevin Belmonte, *Chesterton's Tavern*, p. 86)

In the passage Belmonte was describing, he was talking about how these men were operating on the "same fundamental moral plain." In short, despite their differences, they were all operating within a broad Christian framework.

Belmonte also quotes Chesterton defending his friend, George Bernard Shaw, but in a way that pays high albeit oblique honor to Bunyan. How this came about was more than a little odd. A story was going around that Shaw had somehow claimed that he, Shaw, was a better writer than Shakespeare, which, had he said it, would have been kind of out there. But Chesterton notes that Shaw had actually said that *Bunyan* was superior to Shakespeare. Shaw took a dim view of Shakespeare because he thought he was living the life of a "disappointed voluptuary," while Bunyan accepted life as a "high and harsh adventure."

> According to this view Shakespeare was always saying, "Out, out, brief candle," because his was only a ballroom candle; while Bunyan was seeking to light such a candle as by God's grace should never be put out. (As quoted in Belmonte, *Chesterton's Tavern*, pp. 84-85)

Chesterton was not the kind of man who could tolerate anyone who was just copping a pose, but he had high admiration for anyone who was genuinely heroic—and Bunyan certainly fits that bill.

Many things go into this, but I would speculate that one of the reasons for it is that Chesterton, like many talented men, had an eye that could identify and appreciate talent and genius. A man like Chesterton would have been able to identify a fellow member of that guild. Thomas Peters notes this about Chesterton:

> Though he claimed mastery in none of the arts, Chesterton was in fact a respectable writer of songs, poetry, drama, essays, short stories, and novels, as well as an accomplished illustrator and cartoonist. (Peters, *The Christian Imagination*, p. 13)

With Bunyan, the list did not include illustrations and cartoons (at least that we know of), but Bunyan also wrote songs, poetry, allegory, sermons, and, just like Chesterton, he did it unencumbered by too much formal education. An apocryphal Mark Twain is purported to have said, "I have never let my schooling interfere with my education." But whether he said it or not, the sentiment applies to *both* Bunyan and Chesterton.

Chesterton had the unique ability to find wonderful things anywhere, and this aptitude could even be extended and applied to a Calvinist like Bunyan. Chesterton was a man in love with the natural world, the world as it stood—the world as it presented itself, and not the world that he or anyone else might have wished to have been. He was a mortal foe of all cant and affectation. It stands to reason that he would find a natural affinity with a man like Bunyan.

> Bunyan stands with Malory and Trollope as *a master of perfect naturalness* in the mimesis of ordinary conversation. (C.S. Lewis, "The Vision of John Bunyan, in *Selected Literary Essays*, p. 146, emphasis mine)

> We must attribute Bunyan's style to *a perfect natural ear*, a great sensibility for the idiom and cadence of popular speech, a long experience in addressing unlettered audiences, and a freedom from bad models. (C.S. Lewis, "The Vision of John Bunyan, in *Selected Literary Essays*, p. 150, emphasis mine)

Chesterton and Bunyan were both imaginative geniuses. And it would have been hard to be an imaginative genius and not be able to recognize one of your peers. Bunyan once spoke of the creative process this way: "and as I pulled, it came." Given the volume of Chesterton's output, something similar had to have been happening to him. He had to know that feeling.

Now of course, because Chesterton knew that Calvinism was the "most non-Christian" of the Christian systems, he would also have to say (and probably did say, somewhere), when encountering someone like Bunyan, that all the good stuff was "in spite of his hard Calvinism," not because of it.

Remember that Chesterton's quite extraordinary gifts were bestowed on a *journalist*. Even though he wrote columns, and articles, he also had a number of side hustles. He wrote novels, poems, detective fiction, theology, and history. But the journalistic framing of all of it is usually pretty evident. When he encounters a phenomenon like Bunyan, he knows how to simply report the story. And it is clear he had a natural affinity for Bunyan's common touch.

T.S. Eliot once described Chesterton's poetry as "first-rate journalistic balladry." From someone of Eliot's genius, his refusal to show contempt for Chesterton's popular touch is noteworthy. At the same time, the readableness of Chesterton is to be remembered. Although Eliot is memorable, he does not even begin to approach Chesterton's lucidity.

Chesterton's ability to wield the machete of clever phrases even carries him through many thickets of his own ignorance. Here is Tolkien writing to his son Christopher about Chesterton's poem *The Ballad of the White Horse*.

> P[riscilla].... has been wading through *The Ballad of the White Horse* for the last many nights; and my efforts to explain the obscurer parts to her convince me that it is not as good as I thought. The ending is absurd. The brilliant smash and glitter of the words and phrases (when they come off, and are not mere loud colours) cannot disguise the fact that G. K. C. knew nothing whatever about the "North," heathen or Christian.

But note that even Tolkien had *previously* thought that it was very good. And it *was* very good, provided you took it the way it was intended.

It is tempting to say that Chesterton never passed up an opportunity to take a swing at Calvinism. But this would not be accurate—he was such a fair-minded man that he could not avoid giving credit where credit was due, even when he was right spang in the middle of being a bigot.

Father Brown
Lends a Hand

Chesterton was a stout Roman Catholic, and not an anemic one. He was a thoroughgoing supernaturalist, and when it came to purported miracles in the history of the church, he was perhaps given to credulity. I think it is fair to say that anyone who thinks that St. Thomas Aquinas levitated once is perhaps given to credulity.

I have not been able to find anything in Chesterton about the Shroud of Turin directly, and so

I defer to my readers on the point. This is called crowd sourcing your research after the book is published. But I would have to confess myself astonished if Chesterton turned out to be anything other than a firm believer in the Shroud—in other words, a believer in the fact that the Shroud of Turin really is the cloth that Christ was buried in, and which bears the image of His body, presumed imprinted on the cloth somehow at the moment of resurrection.

It is therefore ironic that the specifically Chestertonian turn of mind was employed, back in 2005, to demonstrate how something like the Shroud could have been faked in the high Middle Ages, and all without using any form of modern technology.

The reasons for believing that something is really unusual with the Shroud are obvious. The image on the Shroud is a photo negative, and the Shroud dates from centuries before the invention of photography. Not only so, but it is also capable of rendering a 3D image, which would have been well beyond the capacities of some medieval forger. Or so it was thought.

The image is not paint or stain or anything else that is detectable. If it is not the image of

Christ, burned onto the cloth in a resurrection blast, then what is it? Enter Father Brown, come to lend a hand to a Protestant debunker.

There is a basic Chestertonian turn of mind that we are seeking to cultivate in what we are pursuing in our project here in Moscow (that of Chestertonian Calvinism). This is not just limited to his jovial side, but also to his ability to rearrange the pieces, to ask the basic question in a different way, and to see everything right side up through the mysterious and arcane process of turning it upside down.

Here is the story. A number of years ago there was a convergence of two events that resulted in New St. Andrews College making something of an international splash—the first of many, no doubt.

The first element was the fact that my son, Nate Wilson, had an instructor in grad school who was "big into" the Shroud of Turin, considering it as an indisputable proof that Christ rose from the dead. It could serve, or so he thought, as the centerpiece of a powerful apologetic for the Christian faith. This was a theological annoyance for Nate, for scriptural reasons. For example, the Bible describes the Shroud as being made up of two cloths, not one. But if the Shroud was not the burial cloth of Christ, it remains a big mystery. What could possibly have produced such a thing?

The second element was that my wife had given Nate a collection of the Father Brown stories in one volume, which he read while home for Christmas break, a time during which he was also bothering over the problems presented by the Shroud. We remember Nate sitting in our living room, sitting on his hands, puzzling over the Shroud.

What he decided to do in his puzzlement was to drop the problem of the Shroud into a Father Brown story. What would Chesterton do? And this was not quite fair, because it is more than likely that Chesterton would have deployed his considerable gifts in a defense of the authenticity of the Shroud. In fact, as alluded to earlier, I would be willing to put money on it.

Nevertheless ... what would Father Brown say if asked how on earth the image of Christ was applied to the Shroud without leaving any trace of pigment, etc.? And the answer that Father Brown would (obviously) give is that the image was never applied to the cloth. Rather, everything that wasn't the image was *removed* from the cloth.

Now isn't this like saying that Michelangelo carved his magnificent statue of David by getting a huge chunk of marble and cutting away anything that didn't look like David? Cute, but not quite.

Next question: How could he remove color from the linen? Could the sun? He got a dark piece of linen, painted a portrait of Christ on a piece of glass, and he left the linen up on the roof of NSA under the glass. The sun moved overhead, thus creating a 3D image, much like an MRI. The sun bleached the portions where the glass was clear, creating a photo negative, and a spooky image of Christ was created, without the use of any pigments or paints. The resultant image looks very much like the image on the Shroud. It is a photo negative, and a 3D image can be generated from it.

There were many other things to test, which have been validated, and, having been checked, they check out. If you look up the Shroud of Turin and read the Wikipedia entry on it, Nate's thesis has been dubbed the Shadow Shroud theory, which in my view is compelling. But my point in bringing this up . . .

I referred earlier to the technique of viewing the world right side up by means of turning it upside down. This is not an absurdity if you remember that our race has fallen into sin and rebellion,

and we have ways of thinking that have been upside down our entire lives. The ways of the world
are not the ways of the Lord. If we learn how to
turn the proper things upside down, we are perhaps learning the ways of the wise.

> For my thoughts are not your thoughts,
> Neither are your ways my ways, saith the
> Lord. For as the heavens are higher than
> the earth, So are my ways higher than your
> ways, And my thoughts than your thoughts.
> (Isaiah 55:8–9)

Sticking Up
for the Puritans

I n his hatred of Puritanism, Chesterton was standing up for an important moral truth and was making what I regard as a historical mistake. He correctly identified the rancid spiritual nature of the glee that a certain kind of person has in simply prohibiting things, but then makes the mistake of thinking that the historical Puritans were actually like that. I think of Mencken's jibe that Puritanism was "the haunting fear that someone, somewhere, may be happy."

Some people do have precisely that haunting fear, and it is right to reject that disposition with loathing. Chesterton clearly saw this in the kill-joys of his day, but he made the common mistake of calling it Puritanism.

> The old theological Puritan had princi-
> ples. The new enlightened Puritan has only
> prejudices. Puritans of the earlier type re-
> jected the things they really loved because
> they thought them wicked. Puritans of the
> new type reject all the things they happen
> to hate, and then simply call them wick-
> ed. (Marlan, Swan, Rabatin, *More Quotable
> Chesterton*, p. 398)

For many years, one of the things I have most liked to do is stick up for Puritans. If there is ever a contest for "most misrepresented" groups within the history of Christendom, the Puritans will certainly be in the final four, and would probably win the championship. Caricatured as stuffy, priggish, censorious, prim, prudish and more, the Puritans have long been type-cast as the Sour Brethren.

I have written a great deal on how wrong this stereotype is, particularly when we are considering the early Elizabethan Puritans. At the same time, the caricature was not manufactured out of whole cloth—from Shakespeare's Malvolio to Hawthorne's Rev. Dimmesdale, the caricature was aimed at *something*. But what was that something?

Here is a tentative suggestion for those who are willing to work with me for a bit. There are many parallels between the Puritans and the Pharisees, even down to what their names meant. The Puritans wanted to purify the Church of England of its remaining popish tendencies. The word *Pharisee* comes from the Hebrew word that means to "set apart" or to "separate." Even to this day, strict evangelical churches teach and insist on a "separated life." The names of both groups therefore indicate their deep desire for holiness, and to make something holy is to consecrate it or set it apart.

Both Puritanism and Pharisaism started as reform movements that were desperately needed in their time. The first Pharisee was quite possibly Ezra, and, if so, this means that they had a long and honored history before they got themselves all tangled up in their scruples. The Puritans were the same—at the beginning, their work was liberating, a breath of fresh air. This is what I would call Chestertonian Puritanism. But after a century or so, something bad began to happen. That "bad" development was seized on by the Puritans' enemies to provide material to over-emphasize and taunt them with. Those along with over-emphasizing those traits, and those same traits were also seized upon by certain members within the Puritan party who decided for various reasons to embrace the caricature.

All this is related to a third point, which is that one of the central aims of the Pharisees was the goal of getting all Israelites to live in accordance with the requirements of the law for priests. One of the central aims of the Puritans was to take the consecration of the monastery and extend it throughout the entire commonwealth. The Pharisees wanted every Israelite to be as holy as the priests. The Puritans wanted every Englishman to be as holy as the monks . . . much holier than the monks, in fact.

Think of the Puritan settlements in America as attempts to build monastic communities where marital sex was encouraged and permitted. But the problem is that wherever there is sex, there will be children, and where there are children, there are subsequent generations. The old-style monastery perpetuated itself by means of recruits, which means that there was much slower organic development over time. But children necessarily accelerate this process of change. The Puritan project here in America was audacious, and for my money, they got farther with this ambitious aim than any other group in church history. But still, something bad did happen to this project.

What is commonly caricatured as the "puritanical" mentality is actually a mentality that can be found in the church of all ages. You can find this mindset in some of the early fathers, you can find it with Syrian ascetics, you can find it in medieval monasteries, and you can find it (after the first generations) among the Puritans. This religious type of person translates every serious call to holiness into terms it can understand, which is that of being introspective, stuffy, priggish, thin-lipped, censorious, prim, prudish, and more.

Not only does it translate every serious call to holiness into this legalistic straitjacket, but it is *attracted* to every serious call to holiness— with the intention of burying it under a rock pile of rules. If God raises up someone to call the Church back to serious devotion to Him in a particular area, and this call is characterized by all those things that ought always to characterize such a call—joy, peace, love, contentment, laughter, feasting, and more joy—then it can be guaranteed that the joy, peace, love books will be published and distributed, and within a very short period of time, the mirthless will show up prepared to take the whole thing to what they honestly believe to be the next level.

This is what happened to some of the Puritans, and to the reputation of all of them. The first Puritans really were liberated. They were seriously joyful, which is a form of being serious, I suppose. And because they wanted their whole nation to experience this joy, and they were *total* Christians, they brought the words of Christ to bear on everything. Their joy was infectious, their talents prodigious, and their logic unanswerable. *At the center of their greatness was a greatness with words, prose and poetry both.*

They carried everything before them, but before you could blink, they found themselves being represented by other "Puritans" who were recognizable in the popular caricature. By the middle of the 17th century, there were two kinds of Puritans, a mixed multitude. There were the free men and there were the gnat-stranglers. But the gnat-stranglers were not the Puritans' unique contribution to the history of religious pathologies—rather, they were a garden variety religious weed that eventually began growing in the Puritans' garden, just as they had grown in every Christian garden up to that point.

Chesterton loathed that kind of fastidious-ness, which he was right to do, but falsely at-tributed that demeanor to Puritans across the board, which was his historical mistake. At one point, he has Father Brown speak about a man's need for squeezing "out of his soul the last drop of the oil of the Pharisees," which is an arduous task. But the Puritans as a class were no more given to this vice than other Christian groups, and for the first century or more of their exis-tence they were a whole lot less given to it. Those who did have a big struggle with it were the early Christian ascetics, men who were ably explained by Chesterton in his book *The Everlasting Man*. And the Puritans would never have dreamed of making Father Brown take a vow of lifelong celibacy in order to serve as a minister. I mean, where did *that* come from?

I have said that the Puritans were great, and that their greatness included a greatness with words. This kind of claim is easily dismissed by those who those been entirely persuaded by the caricatures, but it cannot be dismissed by anyone who is willing to consider the historical facts. It is true that the poetaster Michael Wigglesworth was a best-selling poet among the New England Puritans, but do we really want to judge the literary merits of any group or any age by means of the popular fads and bestsellers? What would become of us as judges in such a case, we who exalt books like *Twilight* and *Fifty Shades of Grey*, and who have not even had a bestselling poet since the time of Kipling?

If we were to name Puritan poets of the first rank, we find we are looking at some of the finest poets that our *culture* has ever produced, men like Spenser, Milton, Herbert, and more.

But before mentioning any other names, I have to say a word about terminology. In the sixteenth century, the term *Calvinism* likely referred to your doctrine of the sacraments, while today it refers to your views of predestination. Thus Hooker was not a Calvinist in their sense, but he was in ours. Herbert was a churchman, happily established in the Elizabethan settlement, but he was a Calvinist in our sense. In a similar fashion, the word *Puritan* referred in their time to those who wanted to reform the liturgy, getting rid of all popish rags, but today it can be aptly applied to anyone who was robustly Protestant and Calvinistic (our sense).

Such literary lights that can be thrown into the mix are those who are acknowledged as great cultural voices (Tyndale, Spenser, Milton, Herbert, Donne, Marvell, Sidney, et al.), others who are seen as minor representatives (Taylor, Bradstreet), and those who are (in my view) unjustly disparaged (Bunyan). Then there are others whose theological underpinnings are ambiguous, thus enabling Protestants and Catholics to fight over the body of Shakespeare. But however you examine it, the Protestant Reformation in the English speaking world was the location, the context, and the setting, of a literary supernova.

There are those who argue that when Calvinism produces works of literary genius, it is "in spite of" the theology, and when it doesn't, it is "because of" that theology. When this happens, we are operating in the comfortable zone of "heads I win, tails you lose."

I would like to spend the rest of my time citing others who have observed some of these same realities, making a few comments of my own as we go. For some, this might seem like a rock pile of quotations, but given the delightful and surprising nature of what is being said, I have no trouble asking you to bear with me.

What were some of the first indications that a literary storm was brewing?

> But on almost any view, Tyndale who inaugurated, and the Genevan translators who first seriously advance, our tradition, tower head and shoulders above all others whom I have yet mentioned. (C.S. Lewis, *English Literature in the 16th Century*, p. 211)

This was not something that was occurring in a separated realm from the foment caused by the Reformation.

> Many surrendered to, all were influenced by, the dazzling figure of Calvin . . . The fierce young don, the learned lady, the courtier with intellectual leanings, were likely to be Calvinists. When hard rocks

of Predestination outcrop in the flowery
of the *Arcadia* or the *Faerie Queen*, we are
apt to think them anomalous, but we are
wrong. The Calvinism is as modish as the
shepherds and goddesses. (C.S. Lewis, *English Literature in the 16th Century*, p. 43)

The nature of the Protestant literary out-
pouring came from the fact that the gospel (understood in the ancient sense of *good news*) had
broken loose and was out in the streets. And
this is a good place to bring in an observation I
have cited before.

But there is no understanding the period of
the Reformation in England until we have
grasped the fact that the quarrel between
the Puritans and the Papists was not primarily a quarrel between rigorism and indulgence, and that, in so far as it was, the
rigorism was on the Roman side. On many
questions, and specially in their view of the
marriage bed, the Puritans were the indulgent party; if we may without disrespect so
use the name of a great Roman Catholic,
a great writer, and a great man, they were

much more Chestertonian than their adversaries. (C.S. Lewis, *Selected Literary Essays*, p. 116)

The theological currents were not just consistent with the literary production but were incorporated into it.

Similarly, William H. Halewood argues that the pervasive Augustinianism of the period—Augustine as interpreted by the Reformation—led Donne, Herbert, Vaughan, Marvell, and Milton to develop a poetic mode exploring man's radical sinfulness and God's overpowering grace. (Lewalski, *Protestant Poetics*, p. 14)

Not only so, but we can shatter several caricatures at once. The Puritans are not only thought of by moderns as cultural Philistines, but also as sexually repressed. This is not only "inadequately true," it is a resounding lie. Speaking of Edmund Spenser, Osgood says this:

The point is that in those particular sonnets which all agree were addressed to Elizabeth

> Boyle, and supremely in his *Epithalamion*, the greatest wedding song in the world, he sings with the same full-throated ease, the same happy assurance that we hear in the contemporary and mature *Hymn of Heavenly Love* and *Hymn of Heavenly Beauty*. (Osgood, *Poetry as a Means of Grace*, pp. 61-62)

Lewis makes the same or a very similar point:

> This antithesis, if once understood, explains many things in the history of sentiment, and many differences, noticeable to the present day, between the Protestant and the Catholic parts of Europe. It explains why the conversion of courtly love into romantic monogamous love was so largely the work of English, and even of Puritan, poets. (C.S. Lewis, *Selected Literary Essays*, p. 117)

The Puritans were not only good poets, they were also *sensual* poets. In his book, *God's Altar*, Daly makes a similar point.

> We can, however, examine Puritan appeals to both the sensuous and the sensual in

man. Such an examination reveals that one who believes that Puritans avoided sensuous and even erotic imagery in expressing religious doctrine or describing spiritual states does so in the face of considerable evidence to the contrary. (Daly, p. 22)

Relief and buoyancy are the characteristic notes . . . It follows that nearly every association which now clings to the word *puritan* has to be eliminated when we are thinking of the early Protestants. Whatever they were, they were not sour, gloomy, or severe; nor did their enemies bring any such charge against them . . . For More, a Protestant was one 'dronke of the new must of lewd lightnes of minde and vayne gladness of harte' . . . Protestantism was not too grim, but too glad, to be true . . . Protestants are not ascetics but sensualists. (C.S. Lewis, *English Literature in the 16th Century*, p. 34)

But we are still not done. Another caricature is that the Puritans were stodgy, didactic, pedestrian. But no—they were sophisticated in their use of symbolism and imagery.

For the Puritan, however, the world in which
he lived was symbolic. Things meant . . . Puritan poets *saw* symbols in the Bible and
the world. From these sources they derived
not only most of their symbols, but the
symbolic method itself, the lens through
which they perceived and expressed their
own experience. Not ornaments retrospec-
tively imposed upon a simple narration,
the Puritan's symbols were central to their
writings because they were central to their
lives. (Daly, pp. 30-31)

Puritan poets . . . knew that part of their
work in this world was to wean their affections from the unmixed love of it. But they
also knew that this world was God's metaphor for His communicable glories and that
another part of their duty was to see and utter that metaphor, to use the figural value
of this world to turn their attentions and
affections to the next. (Daly, p. 81)

Some have been misled by the fact that there
was an iconoclastic element to the Reformation, which there certainly was. But it was not

a case of banishing images and replacing it all with nothing. It was a case of banishing certain kinds of images and replacing them with images that many people are not sophisticated enough to understand.

> We are quite rightly impressed by the icon-oclastic dimensions of the Reformation, the pruning of the liturgies and the decimation of the saints' days, the removal of statues, paintings and even stained glass from the churches. But such iconoclasm may be eclipsed by what we can call the iconopoaic energies of the Reformation, its creativity in producing new allegories and metaphors for the divine and the human which, by their novel connections and collocations, bedded together the hitherto incompatible and subverted one cosmos while paving the way for another . . . When your metaphors change, your world changes with them. (Matheson, pp. 6-7)

Given the high view of Scripture, it is natural that the Protestant aesthetic gravitated toward the written word. This partly explains why many

STICKING UP FOR THE PURITANS   133

moderns think that a Protestant aesthetic never happened at all.

> We should, however, approach Augustinian aesthetics not in medieval but in Reformation terms, taking account of the important new factor introduced by the Reformation—an overwhelming emphasis on the written word as the embodiment of divine truth. In this milieu the Christian poet is led to relate his work not to ineffable and intuited divine revelation, but rather to its written formulation in scripture. The Bible affords him a literary model which he can imitate in such literary matters as genre, language, and symbolism, confident that in this model at least the difficult problems of art and truth are perfectly resolved. My proposition is, then, that far from eschewing aesthetics for a rhetoric of silence or a deliberate anti-aesthetic strategy, these poets committed themselves to forging and employing a Protestant poetics, grounded upon scripture, for the making of Protestant devotional lyrics. (Lewalski, *Protestant Poetics*, pp. 6-7)

I mentioned earlier that it is *de rigueur* to think contemptuously of Bunyan, a man of true literary genius, and someone who was Protestant to his back teeth. So, allow me to finish with a few observations about him from Lewis, and then from Chesterton.

> But this fault is rare in Bunyan—far rarer than in *Piers Plowman*. If such dead wood were removed from *The Pilgrim's Progress* the book would not be very much shorter than it is. The greater part of it is enthralling narrative or genuinely dramatic dialogue. Bunyan stands with Malory and Trollope as a master of perfect naturalness in the *mimesis* of ordinary conversation. (C.S. Lewis, *Selected Literary Essays*, p. 146)

> We must attribute Bunyan's style to a perfect natural ear, a great sensibility for the idiom and cadence of popular speech, a long experience in addressing unlettered audiences, and a freedom from bad models. (C.S. Lewis, *Selected Literary Essays*, p. 150)

The high view that Lewis takes of Bunyan's abilities is perhaps well known. Perhaps a little more surprising would be these tributes from Chesterton.

> *The Pilgrim's Progress* certainly exhibits all the marks of such a revival of primitive power and mystery . . . Nowhere, perhaps except in Homer, is there such a perfect description conveyed by the use of merely plain words. (Quoted in Belmonte, p. 205)

> Before the Puritans were swept off the scene for ever, they had done two extraordinary things. They had broken to pieces in plain battle on an English meadow the chivalry of a great nation, bred from its youth to arms. And they had brought forth from the agony a small book, called *The Pilgrim's Progress*, which was greater literature than the whole contemporary culture of the great Renaissance, founded on three generations of the worship of learning and art. (Belmonte, p. 206)

To reapply Chesterton from another context, there are certain things a man might want to oppose, but honesty would constrain him to do it without patronizing. And I would argue that the monuments to Puritan literary achievements should be, *at the very least*, in that category.

> Reformation was less a shopping-list of demands than the choreography for a new dance. (Matheson, p. 9)

All of this has applications for our own time.

> The new vogue for dialogue, satire and narrative history gave priority to story-telling, to the *via rhetorica* over the *via dialectica*; conversation, intuition and empathetic imagination took over from logic, paradox from syllogism, open disputations in the 'public square' from magisterial pronouncements behind closed doors. These are not just matters of style and form. They point to a fundamentally new way of perceiving and presenting the truth. (Matheson, *The Imaginative World of the Reformation*, p. 28)

When the Reformation broke out, as Matheson argues persuasively, it was *a revolution of the imagination*. It was not a matter of one dusty scholastic replacing another, but rather scholastic bores being replaced by the poets and prophets. This state of affairs describes wonderfully the first century (more or less) of the Reformation. Elizabethan Puritans, Tyndale, Luther, and countless others—these men were *alive* to the grace of God in everything; they were holy, and mischievous. Read over Matheson's description of the Reformation again. Dialogue. Satire. Narrative. Storytelling. Imagination.

Whatever would we do if the *spirit* of the reformation broke out once again in our Reformed churches of today? I suspect that the curators would do everything in their power to get it all back into the museum cases. If there were to be another Reformation today, who would be the dialecticians resisting it? Who would be the imaginative poets promoting it? What would they be called? What would they be called three centuries after the fact?

God as Good Author

M any people struggle with the problem of evil. If God is all powerful, then he could elimi-nate evil. If God is all good, then He should certainly want to. So then why does the classic Christian position teach us that God is both all-powerful *and* all good, and yet evil con-tinues to exist?

> Again, the kingdom of heaven is like unto treasure hid in a field; the which when a man hath found, he hideth, and for joy

thereof goeth and selleth all that he hath,
and buyeth that field. (Matt. 13:44)

Before getting to that exciting topic, let us first
work through this short little parable, and sum-
marize it.

What is the kingdom like? It is like hidden
treasure. When a man finds it, he then hides it
again, and in his joy, he goes and sells everything
in order to buy that field. This is a *kingdom* mystery—which means it is like that purloined letter
in Poe's mystery.

The treasure in this instance is hidden in
plain sight. The seller gives it all up, not knowing
the value of what he is giving up. The buyer relin-
quishes everything he has elsewhere in order to
obtain that which has value beyond all reckoning.

So who is the seller here? I take it to be the nation of Israel, not knowing the value of their field,
or the treasure contained within it. Although
they did not know the value, their ignorance was
culpable. They *ought* to have known. The buyer—Gentiles from east and west—abandons all
he used to have, gives it up, and comes into his
new possession, well knowing the value of what
he now has. Thus far the point of the parable.

But after that point, I want to step back a few paces and look at the mere *fact* of the parable. Realize that the gospel itself is just such a lost treasure story.

We are talking about gospel story, the story of the gospel, and story gospel.

"The kingdom of God is like a man who . . ." Time is mysterious, space is mysterious, people are mysterious, and story arcs are mysterious. In order to have a story that is *interesting*, there must be conflict. Moreover, there must be conflict once upon a time.

Perhaps we should qualify this by saying that in order for story in *this* world to be interesting, there has to be conflict. Presumably, we won't be bored in Heaven, and we also know that in the resurrection the kind of warfare that we now undergo has ceased. "Her warfare has been accomplished" (Is. 40:2). If the millennial age is one in which the swords are fashioned into plowshares, how much more will this be true of the eternal state (Micah 4:3)?

But in order to keep from becoming bored with all that everlasting peace and harmony, there must be a placeholder for that conflict. What will take the place of sinful conflict in the eternal state?

In our resurrected and glorious condition, there will be no suffering, tears, bloodshed, or anything else like that. But there will be *something*. We just don't know what it is yet.

My nomination for that post is a little something called *difficulty*. Maybe God will assign you to the planet Jupiter, and charge you to grow giant turnips there, fifty feet across. But all that is just speculation. Speculation, you say. No kidding? But we do know that the resurrection life will be perfect, and that does mean *not boring*.

We are grappling with what constitutes perfect storytelling.

Whether or not the stories themselves grow increasingly gripping, we know that *storytelling* will finally come into its own. Perhaps the solution to this dilemma is found in the fact that in the resurrection, the glorious things that God accomplished *here* will finally find a narration *there* that is worthy of the subject.

> And I beheld, and I heard the voice of many angels round about the throne and the beasts and the elders: and the number of them was ten thousand times ten thousand, and thousands of thousands; Saying

with a loud voice, *Worthy is the Lamb that was slain* to receive power, and riches, and wisdom, and strength, and honour, and glory, and blessing. (Rev. 5:11–12)

God knows how to stack one choir upon another, and so myriads of angels will ascend on the celestial risers. And there they sing about the crucifixion, about something that happened here, in *this* life, in our history.

But if they are singing about the worth of the Lamb who was slain, then that means that they will be singing about God's glorious purposes regarding the murder of His Son.

As we ask *Why evil?*, we need to remember that in the perfections of Heaven, evil will be *remembered*. It will be remembered, gloriously, perfectly.

Thinking about this, we need to make sure that we are not falling prey to a misconceived analogy. If you were making the perfect salad, you would take the garden slug out of it. If you were making the perfect wine, you would make sure to remove the battery acid. If you were decorating the living room perfectly, you would take the greasy engine block off the coffee table. If you were making the perfect flower arrangement, you would not drape a dirty bicycle chain over the vase. But we are in danger of becoming the victim of our analogies.

Now . . . if you were telling the perfect story, would you remove the evil from it? Think for a moment. Would it have improved *The Lord of the Rings* if Tolkien had left out Sauron? Or Saruman? Or the Nazgul? Or Gollum? With the disappearance of each villain or antagonist, is the story getting progressively better? Or worse?

I suspect that Chesterton's reflexive reaction against Calvinism is the result of a metaphysical mistake, thinking that evil in the world is the slug in the salad instead of thinking of it as the antagonist in the story. I suggest this tentatively because out of all the mistakes that a man like Chesterton might make, that of missing the key element of story would be the very last one. But there it is, and I think he did.

> The kings of the earth stood up, and the rulers were gathered together against the Lord, and against his Christ. For of a truth against thy holy child Jesus, whom thou hast anointed, both Herod, and Pontius

Pilate, with the Gentiles, and the people
of Israel, were gathered together, For to do
whatsoever thy hand and thy counsel determined before to be done. (Acts 4:26–28)

God is the good author of the good story.
God is the perfect author of the *perfect* story.
God freely and unalterably ordains whatsoever
comes to pass . . .

Yet so as thereby neither is God the author
of sin, nor is violence offered to the will of
the creatures, nor is the liberty or contin-
gency of second causes taken away, but
rather established. (WCF 3.1)

God is not the author of sin, but He most certainly is the author of a story that has sin *in* it.
This is not a defect in the story but is rather one
of the central glories of it.

The story of our redemption from the Fall will
be the bloom of a fallen creation. When the day
of resurrection finally comes, it is not the case
that God has mighty angels pick up big erasers
in order to wipe out everything that had gone before. The cosmos is not erased, and the history of

the cosmos is not erased. The cosmos is reborn,
and what went before is contained within, and
glorified by, that new and resurrected state.

> Because the creature itself also shall be
> delivered from the bondage of corruption
> into the glorious liberty of the children of
> God. For we know that the whole creation
> groaneth and travaileth in pain together un-
> til now. (Rom. 8:21–22)

> Therefore, my beloved brethren, be ye st-
> edfast, unmoveable, always abounding in
> the work of the Lord, forasmuch as ye know
> that *your labour is not in vain* in the Lord. (1
> Cor. 15:58)

Long Live the West

As we pause to reflect on what is wrong with our civilization, I hope I have shown the need to turn to Chesterton, and I would urge us to resort to one of the best things he ever said— and that is saying something. But you will have to wait a few more moments for it.

We live in a time when we are *constantly* reminded of the sins of the West. I do not wish to deny the reality of such sins, and still less to deny the gravity of them—at least if we are talking about the sins that actually happened, as opposed to those that the progressives have simply made up out of their own heads.

But if we are talking about the real sins, I do want to place them in a different light than they usually get, under a different glass. I want to do this because a commitment to truth demands it, and on top of everything else, it is a matter of great *strategic* import.

A particular play is being run on us, and almost no one seems to be aware of the nature of that play. And so, with that concern in mind, there are three things I would like to ask you to consider. If you walk away from this chapter with these three points in mind, I will be content.

The first is that the West must not be defined by her secularism. Secularism is not the genius of the West but is rather the disease of the West. I have been urging Christians of all stripes to return to an older method of cultural organization, one that is much hardier than what we are currently attempting. Every culture is an instantiation of a particular set of faith commitments, and those faith commitments must either be (what people of previous generations would have in their simplicity called) true or false.

Not to put too fine a point on it, the reason our culture is demented is that our gods are demented. The reason we have lost our minds is the direct result of losing our faith in God, and we have sought after gods that stand for no objective truth whatever.

> For my people have committed two evils; they have forsaken me the fountain of living waters, and hewed them out cisterns, broken cisterns, that can hold no water. (Jer. 2:13)

Our self-made cisterns hold no water, and this is why our worldview *holds no water*. Our secularist overlords might act a little indignant at such a saying, muttering that we Christians are the ones who are anti-science. Yeah, right. You think little boys can become little girls, and you think *we're* anti-science? Why don't you turn a bull into a cow first, and then we can talk about your science.

Keep in mind there are only three basic options on the table. The first is an etiolated and diseased secularism, one that we have been repeatedly told is "progressive." But it is not progressing anywhere unless, to use Van Til's apt phrase, we decide to count its "integration downward into the Void."

Their basic strategy will be to continue to gaslight those Christians who are warning about the future, saying that they are paranoid, and then, when all the prophecies start coming true, they will move seamlessly into saying that it is not realistic to try to do anything about it now.

The second option is that of Islam, filling up the vacuum created by retreating and outbred secularists (and the Christians who continue for some reason to believe the reassurances of those retreating and outbred secularists). Whatever else it is, the ideology of having 1.2 children per household is not a vision for a workable future.

The third option is what I have been calling mere Christendom. There will be no salvation for us without a Savior, and one of the things our Savior wants us to do is *name* Him, to call upon Him. He is not deaf. *Call* on Him.

So my first point is that Christian civilization—a true Christian civilization—is a good thing. A genuinely good thing. Not only is it a good thing, it is also a possible thing. Think for a moment. Something that existed for a thousand years ought not to be called an *impossible* thing, right? And that leads to the second point.

The second issue is that there is a vast difference between being attacked *for* your sins and being attacked *with* your sins. There is no denying that we believers have failed in many considerable ways, and so it is easy for Christians with a tender conscience to believe that our critics are being sincere when they chide us for our sins. But they are not at all sincere. They hate us for our virtues, and they attack us *with* our sins, not *for* our sins.

David the king provides us with a good example of this. He was hated by the enemies of God because he was a man after God's own heart—and yet that tragic business with Bathsheba did give the drunkards in taverns something to sing about. And sing about it they did. And the late-night comedians went on and on about it.

Lot in Sodom is another example. Peter in the New Testament calls him a righteous man, and yet in the Genesis account we see exactly how his various compromises had rendered him vulnerable to grievous temptations.

This is no reason to go on sinning—of course not. Sin does a lot of damage. Christians, by means of their sins, manage to blow up families, friendships, businesses, churches, denominations, and so forth, and then they want to run America? Try running a successful shaved ice stand first. There's *that* principle. You are going to be attacked for your virtues, and not for your sins. But when you sin, you supply the enemy with free ammo. Why are you giving the enemy free ammo?

But back to the point. When we consider the various dirty deeds that tarnish our past—broken treaties, needless wars, you know the drill—always remember that these are all sins that were long ago weaponized. They are *not* what they are being currently represented as being.

The third thing is that we ought not to give up hope—but I want to suggest a counterintuitive reason for this. Do not give up hope because things are far worse than we think. We ought not to give up hope because—and yes you heard me rightly—things really are hopeless.

Chesterton once said this:

> Christendom has had a series of revolutions and in each one of them Christianity has died. Christianity has died many times

and risen again; for it had a God who knew
the way out of the grave. (*The Everlasting
Man*, p. 250)

Things are dire, but that is all right. We can
do dire. Things are hopeless, but in the history
of the West, they have been hopeless *many* times
before. This is like old home week. As the apostle
Paul once put it, God does this so that we would
not trust in ourselves.

But we had the sentence of death in ourselves, that we should not trust in ourselves, but in God which raiseth the dead.
(2 Cor. 1:9)

The pattern of death and resurrection is His
basic m.o. Death followed by resurrection is His
signature move. Allow me to say that again. This
pattern of cultural decline and great reformation
is *His signature move*.

Far too many of us have lamented, together
with the Psalmist, "I have seen the wicked in
great power, and spreading himself like a green
bay tree" (Ps. 37:35). And when the foundations
are destroyed, what can the righteous do (Ps.

11:3)? Their eyes are fat like grease, and their press secretaries lie like dead flies on a window-sill. And they all seem to get *away* with it!

But remember. Our God does know the way out of the grave. And not only does He know the way out of the grave, it has been His plan and intention to govern all of human history by this means. He leads us, *always*, out of the grave. But first it is His glorious intention to bring us *to* that grave, and we must always trust Him as we approach it. He has done this countless times for us. He has done this great thing over and over. This is His move. And that means this is His moment.

I have said this before, and trust that I will have occasion to say it many times again. *The king is dead. Long live the king.* And while there are qualifications I could make here—for western civilization is not the same thing as the king-dom of Heaven—I will pass by all such qualifica-tions in serenity and peace. I do this because all the animus that western civilization draws from the *ignorati* is because it *reminds* them of the kingdom of Heaven. It does not remind them of the policies of Hell. If it reminded them of Hell, they would think much more highly of it.

My three exhortations to you have been these. Secularism is the name of our malaise, the name of our backsliding. We must have a cure for our disease, but our civilization is not our disease. Our civilization has a disease, and the name of it is secularism. So secularism is not the name of our guiding principle. It is not our cornerstone, but rather the corrosion of our capstone. I am not calling for us to throw neutrality away, for you cannot dispense with something you never had. Neutrality is impossible. Not one person ever had neutrality. Our society could jettison neutrality if we had it, but we don't. We can, however, throw away our *pretense* of neutrality. Secularism is something that must be repented of. And as I say this, do not confuse it with religious liberty. Religious liberty was a Christian invention. Secularism was a Christian apostasy.

Our fundamental confession as Christians is that *Jesus is Lord*. Our confession is *not* that He is Lord someplace else. We are not proclaiming His authority over Heaven. Neither are we limiting His realm to our hearts.

Second, we must confess our sins, and we can tell we have done so if we receive forgiveness for them. You know that you are dealing with the

Holy Spirit when you confess sin, because His whole point in convicting you is to bring you into peace. You know that you are dealing with devils, with accusers, when you "confess sins," as defined by them, because their whole point in bringing them up is to bury you in successive waves of condemnation.

What was actually an oceanic enormity centuries ago has dribbled down to a small puddle made up of micro-aggressions. Micro-aggressions are to real sin what LaCroix is to fruit juice. And that is what we are told we must feel bad about, right alongside our current oceanic enormities—things like same-sex mirage, abortion-on-demand, and the redefinition of "theft as generosity" that socialism attempts.

And last, God saves the helpless. God can always save the helpless. The West is helpless. The West is dead. Long live the West.

Made in the USA
Coppell, TX
02 December 2023

25198592R00095